1

BARTERED LIVES

BARTERED LIVES

Love and Betrayal in North India

JOYSHRI LOBO

PARTRIDGE
A Penguin Random House Company

To order additional copies of this book, contact
Partridge India
000 800 10062 62
orders.india@partridgepublishing.com

www.partridgepublishing.com/india

Contents

For...

Ozzie my husband,

sons Jayant, Rohit, Raoul,

their soul-mates Charu, Tanu and Deidra,

all of who are reflected in these pages.

My grand-children Dhruv, Ronan and Ronika,

who I depend on to create a more equal world.

Also in fond memory of my parents,

Monu and Sharda Dutt,

whose inter-faith marriage set the canvas

for the colours of this book,

and Stella, the clownish cocker spaniel,

whose antics are legendary.

CHAPTER I

"Unless a tree has borne blossoms in spring, you will vainly look for fruit on it in autumn."... Hare.

UNEQUAL STATIONS

"Why does she run around like a new born colt on unsteady legs?" Gulabo asked as she watched the young Memsahib through a narrow, soot-covered glass pane in the kitchen. Her mother Durgi left the washing at the sink and joined her to look at Shakuntala, known by the shorter nickname of "Shaku," in the Baksh family.

"Because she is a tom-boy and an only child!" snapped the mother. "The Maalik, our master, spoils her silly and the Maalkin, does not know how to control her. If they had a son, all would have been well."

Durgi's comments were based on her own experience. She blamed herself entirely for having produced three daughters while trying for a son. Her husband and in-laws never failed to blame her for the inadequate performance, and let up on nagging only after the birth of her youngest child, a son, Ravi.

"I wish I was like her," Gulabo sighed. "No clothes to pound or utensils to wash... just a little reading and writing and hot meals served at the table. Have you noticed the Maalkin's finger-nails? Rounded to perfection and lacquered daily to match her sari. Look at my hands!" She spread out the offending appendages, in disgust. The nails were bitten into jagged ends as grease and ash blackened the fingertips. They were calloused hands, rough and too old in comparison to their young, fourteen year old owner. She picked up the green slab of dish detergent and tried to wash away the dirt. The caustic soda only made her skin drier and caused painful splits in the finger tips.

"Can't we use a better soap?" she grumbled.

"You get back to kneading dough for the Maalik's breakfast! At least we know our place... and don't you get any strange ideas looking at the young Memsahib. As for better soaps... what's wrong with this? Besides I do bring home the slivers they throw out. Nothing ever satisfies you three girls. Ravi might be an improvement!"

"Don't be angry Amma... I was just thinking aloud. Life is so unfair! Why did God create different castes? Will I ever be as free and rich as her?"

"Your father and I did not raise you to think for yourself or question the rightness or wrongness of our lot! The thinkers are rebels, parasites, the non-workers, the real outcasts of society. A permanent government job, and the money it brings, commands respect. The less cash you have the more you will be kicked around. Remember that my girl! Thinkers grumble, ask too many questions and are a disgruntled lot. They fight against the system. Our caste dictates that we stay within the circle created by our destiny as a result of our ancestors' Karma."

"Karma!" mumbled Gulabo in exasperation. Every sorrow and deprivation in the family was always explained away through Karma, or action and reaction followed by rewards or punishment.

"Yes Karma!" emphasized Durgi. "If we do not acknowledge this great law, we become like the washer man's dog who belongs neither at the river nor in the house. 'Dhobi ka kutta na ghar ka na ghat ka.' I don't ever want to become that kind of street dog. The day any one of us does, we shall be out under the flyovers. Even today we are the puppets of the upper castes, however much that old man Gandhi tried to change things."

"They say he was a great man, Amma, our Bapu. If he was alive today, most of us would be working with government, not as ill-paid domestics in homes."

"I don't know who fills your head with useless thoughts. Nothing will ever change. Government indeed! Can it change attitudes?"

Gulabo had a faraway look in her eyes. She persisted... "If... just think of it... if the Father of the nation, Gandhi was alive today, I could marry anyone, even an Amreekan! Isn't that so Amma?"

11

"So you would like to believe! We are to be used... such marriages are not for us..." there was an angry edge and a tinge of hopelessness in Durgi's voice as she looked back at her own dreary existence. "You are old enough now. On a day the priest considers auspicious, you shall marry your cousin Ramu. It is all arranged with your Maamu, my brother. Till then you must follow our ways and be a good and obedient child. Young Memsahib's conduct is most unseemly."

"I don't like Ramu. He is mean and weeps at the slightest excuse. Do you remember when he pulled my veil and it caused abrasions around my throat? I did not cry, but when I hit him in return, he wept copiously and tattled to Maamu, who screamed his head off at me! What sort of husband will he make?"

Durgi, used to being the alpha female in her family, hated back-chat and pulled hard at her daughter's plait. The child winced. "Not another word from you! You will learn to live with that boy. How can we find dowries for three daughters if each one wants to choose her own husband? Your Maamu will not expect a big dowry. That is important, not your filmy stories. And when Ravi marries, he shall bring back all the money we spent on you. That is the custom. Bring sons into the world and pay back comes in the form of his bride and her 'dehej,' all the worldly goods she will need in the new home. Produce daughters and we lose what-ever we already have. Pity Ravi is so young! It will be a long time before a daughter-in-law will come to take over the work from me. God was unkind in giving me daughters first. I long to put up my feet like the Maalkin. Ravi's wife will wait on me hand and foot, if I don't meet my Maker before that!Hai Bhagwan... why don't you relieve me this life soon?" She looked upwards towards the roof, hands folded.

Gulabo was used to her mother's tirades. She was a strong woman both physically and mentally. She must have been beautiful too, but now had a constant sneer. Nothing seemed to please her, especially not the sight of her three daughters, who were a constant reminder of an expensive future, brought on by the dowries that would have to be paid out to prospective husbands. And, without marriage, no woman's life was considered complete.

"I shall make enough money for my own dehej!" Gulabo assured her.

"With your face you just might!" said Durgi indulging her daughter with a rare smile. "Your mausi, my sister Savitri, took off the gold bangles from her wrists and sold them to buy the specified number of saris for Pinky. It was a shame as no woman should have to part with her istridhan, the wealth that she brings from her home. It is the only security she has in the in-laws house. They might even kill her, but for that!"

An uneasy silence prevailed in the kitchen as Durgi sat on her haunches, stoking the charcoal fire that heated a heavy black skillet in readiness for stuffed parathas to be served at the Bari Kothi for breakfast. She looked at her first born. Green eyes, sharp nose, heavy eye-brows shaped like a crow's wings and a skin of the lightest golden honey. Even if the marriage did not take place, there would be many men hovering around her like hungry bees. She was not too concerned about Gulabo's future. With looks like these, she would make it in life. It was Khamo and Ruby, she was worried about. They had their father Hira's flat, dull looks and dark colouring. Even amongst her caste, boys were getting choosy. The in-laws were even worse. They asked for a fridge, and the last prospective mother-in-law had said patronizingly, "Not too large a fridge sister. A medium size will do, and a scooterette. Plus a little jewelry and cash to start the young couple off in life. Can't appear small before the family and guests, can we?" She was affronted when Durgi silently showed her the door soon after a cup of tea and a plate of laddoos and samosas.

That was why she and Hira had agreed to marry Gulabo to Durgi's brother's son, Ramu. There were two other sons who would be useful in the future. Durgi had made it clear to her brother that there would be minimal dowry, but as he had a productive field of wheat and barley, the girls would prove themselves good and useful workers. They were strong enough to pull the yoke when there were not enough bulls during the sowing season, as Maamu would hire them out on stud duty to the villagers.

Gulabo was the fruit of a one night liaison with a visitor from 'Amreeka.' Durgi did not even know his name. The man was drunk, far from home and lonely. He came to the clinic for treatment. Deepak brought him home to dinner. As Durgi passed the fluffed out phulkas, (the air filled, bloated unleavened bread so popular in the north) she felt a hand touch her thigh. Sex did not depend on language, and she understood that from past experiences. She waited by the gate in the shadow of the jasmine bush, from which she had plucked a few sweet smelling star like flowers for her hair. As he was leaving, she guided him into the 'baradari,' the twelve arched monsoon pavilion created by Vaid Hari Baksh, in the orange garden. The man was too drunk and ill to do anything but Durgi helped him fill a void in a strange country; a country where he had come to teach new farming practices; a country where he fell ill with depressing regularity. Durgi was richer by a hundred dollars, a small fortune in rupees. Her husband Hira, who knew that she earned extra money to supplement a meager income, had drunk himself to sleep, not in sorrow but happy at the thought of a moment's respite from pulling people around in a rickshaw. His groin ached from sitting on a small, hard, black plastic, triangular seat and when Durgi offered him her pendulous breasts in apology that night, the pain and sheer exhaustion of a working day, made him turn away. Food and sleep was all that he required.

- -

Shaku ran into the wind, her long black hair cascading like a dark stream that flowed off her shoulders, down to the waist. When plaited it looked like a twisted snake, supple, glistening, a whiplash of energy, often coiled around her slender neck. She closed her eyes for a moment. The lashes were thick and curled into her eyelids. The light brown eyes were bright with the constant expectation of discovery and excitement. The full, red lips pouted, slightly upturned, often cynical and questioning. With the fair skin of a high caste Brahmin, she made a pretty picture of confident, willful womanhood. She was unusually tall and slender, a precocious child, loquacious and silly in the presence of doting parents but astute in the ways of her generation. She pondered over matters that seemed inexplicable, but more often than not, drew the right conclusions through logical thought and a defiantly independent, rebellious streak.

An impatient flick of the wrist pushed away loose strands of soft, straight hair from the eyes. Red and blue glass bangles tinkled as they collided on her tiny wrists. This was the moment she savoured, running through the fruit trees, as free as the wind on a not-yet-burning summer morning.

As the day advanced, the sun rose in a copper sky, bright enough to cause temporary blindness, hot enough to blacken and parch exposed skin. It forced every living creature in to finding shade beneath leafy trees, behind walls, under roofs, canvas and hay stacks. Even butterflies clustered under the leaves of trees or cooled themselves like tiny yellow sails around the shallow slush pools under the guava tree. All would wait for the blistering orb to go down by the evening, before emerging to cool off in the oft imagined drop in temperature, brought on by the night.

Summer in the Punjab was harsh and often unbearable. Grass mats inter-woven with strands of scented khus-khus and kewra, hung from windows, and were sprayed with water every few hours, to help cool the incoming dry air. It was an effective method, but it ruined the white-washed walls, leaving blistered lime and dark grey-green mildew patches. Vaid Hari Baksh had also put up heavy, frilled, embroidered, curtain-like fans from the roofs in the bedrooms, sitting areas and verandahs. The servants children pulled the ropes for a small remuneration, but often the soporific heat made them drowsy and they would lie down, asleep, to be shouted awake by one of the sweating, irritable occupants of the Bari Kothi, literally 'the large house,' as distinguished from more modest homes and servants quarters in the area. Afternoons were a time to rest and wait out the summer heat. Nobody worked. All India agreed to sleep as a protest against the cruelty of her sizzling, summers.

Shaku bathed in fresh water that poured out of tin pans strung along the Persian wheel. The bull that patiently pulled at the iron rod attached to the wheel, did its mandatory rounds, morning and evening, 365 days a year. Hakim, the bearer's son, sat on the struts, gently coaxing the animal in a soft, sing song voice. Beast and boy looked hewn out of a single stone, timeless like some ancient bas-relief from the pre-historic Ajanta caves. To Shaku, the buffalo boy was an intriguing mystery. She often wove stories around him. He was always silent and powerful in her dreams and rescued her from terrible danger. One of her frequent nightmares was that she was lying in a ditch, blood oozing from her forehead. Hakim would keep trying to breathe life into her mouth but could not do so. It was a terrifying vision. Shaku told no one about it, pushing it out of her mind as the fantasy of an over-imaginative teenager.

As she quickened her pace through the guava orchard, planted fifty years earlier by her grandfather, Vaid Hari Baksh, she glanced at Hakim. Tall, well built, fair, he worked hard and was never seen playing or chatting with the other servants who worked in and around the Bari Kothi. She wished he would smile at her or even glance at her. She chuckled to herself. Hakim sat with down cast eyes whenever she bathed at the well. Her freshly washed hair and wet sari dried as she moved through the orchard.

Pushpa, her mother, often told her that she was a "big girl now" and ought to avoid bathing outside. The hot, northern summer was unbearable and the only time Shaku felt cool was when she bathed at the well and felt the breeze on her wet clothes. This was her summer routine since infancy and she had no desire to change it. She laughed off her mother's fears and continued with her early morning baths in the garden. At night she often sat on the low wall of the well, saw the yellow moon mirrored in the still water, as unblinking frogs floated, waiting for insects to fall onto their sticky tongues. She wondered if Hakim noticed her. He looked sculptured and voiceless, an enigma that needed to be understood.

Shaku hummed as she skipped along. It was a song her mother Pushpa, had often sung to her as a lullaby whenever she was restless and could not sleep. It narrated the story of the Love God Krishna, who went around the luxuriant, green forest looking for cow-girls who flirted and played hide and seek with him. In the cool corridors of the bungalow, Shaku often danced to the song. It epitomized the freedom of youth and infinite generosity of nature.

"Why is Krishanji coloured blue in every calendar and statue?" she asked.

Pushpa was impatient. Her daughter asked too many questions. "Blue depicts a dark but royal skin. He was a Yadav, one of the lower castes."

"And yet we treat them as if they are aliens from another world!" mused Shaku.

"Did he only flirt with the gopis or did matters proceed further?" she asked her mother who was horrified at her daughter's line of thinking. "How can you ask me such a question?"

"Then I'll ask Baba. He will have no qualms about telling me."

- -

"Shaku... come in at once! Have your milk and almonds. I'm not going to heat the milk again!" Pushpa sounded irritable.

Every morning, before breakfast, she gave her family freshly boiled milk and a fistful of blanched almonds. Both were supposed to sharpen the mind and clear the skin. Almonds and cow's milk were the panacea for most ills relating to the mind. Mother and daughter never used soap on their faces. After a gentle but invigorating scrub with a paste made of gram flour and curd, they washed it off with a few drops of fresh milk diluted in water. Their spotless, smooth skins were proof of the efficacy of this particular family recipe.

"Coming Ma! Give me a minute... my sari is still damp." Pushpa did not approve of her daughter's independence or education. The child was tutored at home by a young teacher from the local Government Model School. The lad, who was barely out of his teens, wanted to supplement his paltry sarkaari talab, the education department's stipulated salary. He could not make Shaku do anything against her will. Moreover he was in love with his young pupil but could only fantasize about marrying her. As a part time teacher he barely made enough to pay for his food and lived with his parents to save on rent.

Dr. Deepak Baksh was a rich man with ancestral wealth and land. The fields surrounding the house were his as was a small village on the outskirts of Jullundur. Both had been gifted to his father, Vaid Hari Baksh as a token of appreciation by the Maharajah of Kapurthala. The man was a renowned tippler and suffered from excruciatingly painful gout. Vaid Hari had removed all trace of it with herbs from his garden. That Deepak had returned the holding to the villagers, spoke of his very humane nature.

There was a lot of laughter and very little instruction between the teacher and pupil. As a Saraswat Brahmin, a follower of Saraswati, the goddess of learning and the arts, his was a higher sub-caste. Pandit Prabhu Dev sported a 'bodi,' a heavenly pigtail on his otherwise completely shaven head and a blessed, white, raw cotton string called a 'janaau,' running from shoulder to torso. Both were symbols of his exalted caste. He often reflected and regretted his lack of funds or familial wealth as it prevented him from marrying Shaku, who was of a slightly lower Brahminical order than him. The ancestral teaching profession made his gotra or sub-caste, superior even to the healers and doctors.

One day Shaku cut the string off with scissors, and earned a sharp slap from her mother who knew the unforgiving nature of traditions and rituals. However, the incident did not stop her from tweaking the young Pandit's 'bodi,' followed by the taunting sentence, "Off you go to heaven!"

Pushpa had had a similar education, through a private tutor, but only till class V. She could read Hindi but no English, which she understood but found uncomfortable and an awkward tongue-twister. Deepak insisted his daughter learnt the language which he considered a gateway to the world. He even wanted her to go to college and take up a salaried job thereafter. Pushpa found the idea ridiculous and a waste of time.

"Suppose she is widowed?" asked Deepak. "Would it not be better that she earned and became independent, rather than relied on her in-laws largesse?"

"How can you think of widowhood even before she is married? It is a bad omen!"

Pushpa looked at her daughter, still flitting through the trees. "When will she grow up?" she looked questioningly at Deepak. "You've spoilt her silly and turned her into the son you never had. She ought to learn to cook, manage the home, play the sitar and sing, not read silly books and paint her toe nails red! We ought to be looking for a suitable boy for her. Instead she plays games, pulls the tutor's 'bodi,' and argues like a man. She takes huge ungainly strides. Her arms are muscular, not delicate. Her calves are knotted and hard like wood. She runs on bare feet and eats fruit straight from the trees! Who will marry such an unladylike creature?"

"Leave her alone Pushpa! I would not have her any other way."

"Of course you would not!" grumbled his angry wife. "What would you know about how a woman from a good home should behave."

"Do you mean I come from not-so-good-a-home?"

"No, but you do come from a home that hardly observes proper Hindu rituals. You don't participate in festivals. You only read books and stick to the clinic. What kind of Hindu husband are you?"

"I may not be a perfect Hindu, but I am a good husband, eh Pushpa?"

Deepak took a deep breath and looked out at his daughter. She was the most precious creature in his life. He had wanted a son to carry on the family name. A male child was a man's pride and the only legal heir to his "title," the surname which identified caste, creed and ancestral occupation. A girl left the home and became her husband's property, never to return, except to celebrate a few festivals whenever her in-laws gave her permission to do so.

When Pushpa was going through a difficult labor, the midwife, secure in the knowledge inherited from the women of her family, made her lie on a bed of sand, warmed by a gentle charcoal fire, lit under the string charpoy. His wife's straining body was covered under many folds of a soft, worn out, muslin sari. Some bacteria from the sand entered Pushpa's womb. She was ill for months and barely survived.

Her deeply scarred womb would never bear children again. It was his wife's near death experience that decided Deepak's career in medicine.

"She's like a beautiful bird... free, happy. Look at her flying through the trees! The boys will be there when she is ready for them. Let her live life to the full now. Girlhood is such a brief period! Before we know it, they have become women. Then they leave us forever." There was sadness in Deepak's voice as he looked fondly out of the window at his only child.

"So what's wrong with that?" Pushpa was incredulous. "She's sixteen now. Our parents planned our marriage when we were babies! We've managed haven't we? I have had no regrets whatsoever."

They "managed" in some sort of humdrum fashion. Their families were neighbors, who often visited each other, participated at functions and prayers, and worshipped at the same temple as they belonged to the same caste. It was inevitable that when a son was born to the Baksh's and a daughter, a year later, to the Batra's, the elders would get together to make a match. The astrologers were consulted to see if their star signs matched. They did. Amidst noisy, ecstatic, colorful celebrations, two sleeping children were united in holy matrimony. They were completely unaware of the momentous occasion. Hundreds of invitees acted as witnesses. At a time when photography had not made its appearance in rural India, guests were helpers, attesters and arbitrators.

Relatives arrived a week or more in advance of the wedding date. Arrangements were made for their stay at friends and other relatives homes. For those who could not get rooms, tents and colourful 'shamianas' were put up as protection from the elements. (Years later when Shaku went to Ajanta with a group of teachers, she looked up to see the cave roof carved and painted like a 'shamiana.' The exquisite sculpturing haunted her through its perfection.) Mattresses and sheets were rented out, as were huge utensils and stoves. All congregated at the bride's home for the community meals which were prepared on a contract basis by Kaku Shah, the best 'halwaai,' or sweetmaker in town. As people sat in the garden on dhurees and charpoys, gossip was exchanged, news shared and a good time had by all. The Indian wedding was the most colorful, raucous, looked-forward-to occasion of a life-time. It brought the clans together and kept the family ties going. Later, guests and relatives would judge time according to the weddings they attended, the people they met, the matches that were made, not according to any other calendar. Occasions marked history, not dates.

"I've heard my parents gave a magnificent dowry," said Pushpa with pride. "We are still using those copper vessels and my gold tissue saris are as good as new. I am keeping them for Shaku. That large tin trunk has all the stuff I am collecting for her dowry. The only thing left is the jewelry." She grew more excited every moment as she imagined the great day in the future.

"Stop it Pushpa! Next you will be reading out the wedding menu to me," admonished Deepak. "The only dowry she will ever need is a college degree. She will stand independent and tall and will never have to be afraid of her husband or in-laws."

"What do you have against a proper marriage? It worked out beautifully for us. Our parents were happy. We looked after them well in their old age, and we never did anything to displease them or our Gods. On Karva Chauth, I have fasted for your health, safety and prosperity. My fasting has kept you faithful and kind. What more can a woman ask for?"

Deepak knew it was his own, disciplined mind that had kept him from straying. There had been many occasions, abroad and at home. Vaid Hari Baksh had set a good moral example. Twenty-three lackluster, marital years flashed before his eyes. Pushpa had been brought to his father's home in a gold coloured, wooden palanquin, soon after her first period. The palki was carried by four young men. It had embroidered, gold brocade curtains and a red velvet interior. He had not seen Pushpa since their babe-in-the-lap marriage. As she stepped out of the 'palki,' he realized how delicately beautiful she was, and very, very shy. While neighbors and friends came to peer at them, the girls giggled and his friends made suggestive, vulgar remarks, as was teasingly permitted at any North Indian wedding.

"Tell us how she tasted, sweet or bitter?" said Pritam.

"I told you I'd take you to GB Road for a practice run, but you were too prudish! What's going to happen now?" chuckled Satwant Singh, in mock concern. (It was ironic that he did not remember, the road housing the Red Light area was named after one of the most venerable, pious politicians of early, post independent India.)

The only indication that Pushpa had heard was the deep red colour on her cheeks, and it had nothing to do with the rouge applied at the beauty parlour.

Pushpa and Deepak were pushed into a flower bedecked room, misty and fragrant with smoke wafting from clusters of sandal-wood joss sticks. They sat on the edge of the bed, curtained by garlands of jasmine and marigold. Both were nervous, tongue-tied, not knowing what to do. He was thirteen, she twelve. Neither had had any physical contact with the opposite sex before. They were expected to do their duty and produce sons and daughters through a physical union. Love did not come into the picture. If emotions did make an appearance, so much the better.

They became conscious of prying eyes, snide remarks and idle curiosity on the other side of the bedroom door. Deepak checked all doors and windows just in case some young enthusiast had drilled a hole to peek in. Privacy was not a privilege or an earned luxury. Honeymoons had been made popular by the British, but after the nuptials, more often than not, the entire family accompanied the young couple to whichever lonely spot they headed for, to get better acquainted. The family always came first.

For almost a week Deepak fumbled with his bride's body. She did not help him at all but lay passive and inert. Every morning his mother came in to look at the sheets and then rushed out to whisper to her women friends. When a red stain appeared, Deepak's Maamu shared a bottle of Neera with his drinking companions, and his mother could not stop smiling as she made the traditional, saffron scented, sweets to be distributed amongst the neighbors.

That first week's sense of shame, inadequacy and public embarrassment became a part of Deepak's adult persona. He would apologize at the slightest excuse. He could never understand how something very private was converted into a public spectacle. He vowed to himself that his children would not suffer such humiliation. He was convinced that illiteracy was the cause of such vulgarity and insensitivity.

Deepak looked angrily into Pushpa's eyes. "That's not going to happen to Shaku. She will not have to ever 'manage!' I want her to feel life, enjoy its intensity, live every moment! She is well read and intelligent. I want her to be an equal partner, a soul mate to her husband. I will find her a fine young man who is educated and makes a comfortable, honest living. She will laugh with him and share his interests... after all we did not put her through school to tie her to someone who will not appreciate her!"

Pushpa shook her head in despair. Her husband never ceased to surprise her. "How can you be so unrealistic? In the end she will have to do household chores and produce babies. That is the lot of women. It cannot change whoever her husband might be. Besides, the in-laws expect it."

"My Shaku will be different, and she will be marrying a man, not his parents." There was a faraway look in Deepak's eyes.

"Just wait and see!" was Pushpa's cynical answer.

- -

Hakim used a hoe to break the dry sods that barricaded one of the many drains into the vegetable garden. Water from the well gushed into the beds. Once they were soaked through, he would replace the dirt and guide the channel towards the radishes that crowned the ridges he had made during the planting of seeds. In summer it took just a day for the blistering sun and 'loo,' the hot, mango-ripening wind, to reduce wet soil into hard lumps, which bare hands could not break. In the late afternoon, his father Mustapha worked the Persian wheel while he watered the garden. It was a generous well. The town often suffered acute water shortages. But Doctor Deepak Baksh's family, servants and plants had plenty, thanks to the foresightedness of Vaid Hari Baksh. The old man grew his own curative herbs, but ever since his death, Deepak maintained only the fruit trees and lawns. As a practicing allopath, he did not require the herbs his father's traditional vocation was dependent upon.

Hakim barricaded the brick and cement drain again to channel the frothing liquid towards the tangerines. He squatted on his haunches and thought about young Memsahib. She was a spoilt brat, beautiful, willful, intelligent. He would watch her bathe but never let her catch him doing so. Though her body was invariably draped in a sari, when wet, it clung to the young contours, encouraging forbidden thoughts in his mind... ones that made him blush and for which his father would thrash him if he ever got to know. Hakim tried to be a good Muslim. He followed the teachings of the Quran as best as he could and knelt on his mat, facing Mecca five times a day, praying for guidance and a good life. He hoped one day to boast of the kind of bump his father's forehead sported after years of sincere, concentrated prayer.

The day's watering almost done, Hakim diverted the flow towards the guava trees. He splashed his face with the cool, clear liquid and leaned against the trunk of a tree. Something hit him hard in the small of his back. Startled, he whipped around and found young Memsahib sitting on a branch above, hidden in the leathery foliage as she ate a green guava. Her foot was poised for another kick. Hakim turned his back towards her and walked away.

"You aren't dumb, are you?" Shaku called after him. "I've never heard you speak a word!"

Hakim whipped around and faced her, arms akimbo. "You have no right to kick me even if you are Huzoor's daughter!" His eyes flashed with anger and humiliation.

"I have the right to do anything at all in this house! It is mine. Besides you are my servant"

"I'm Huzoor's servant, not yours. Even that won't last long, for I'll soon leave this place." Hakim walked away as fast as possible and went to join Mustapha at the well.

"Where is the servant boy going?" Shaku asked her mother at the lunch table.

"Your father has some silly notion that Hakim has to be educated at the American Missionary Technical School. He doesn't want him to be a servant."

"No wonder he is so insolent! He does not know his place. He is a servant, isn't he Baba?"

"Did he say something to you?" Pushpa asked.

"Just that he wasn't my servant."

"He isn't young lady," her father confirmed. "None of them are your servants. You'd better learn to treat the staff with respect."

"What will he be taught there?" Shaku asked, curiosity getting the better of her.

"Driving, tractor repair and all the things that are useful around a farm. We need someone to work the fields. He is young, bright and a hard worker. I am sure Bhai comes from a very good family in Afghanistan." By 'good' Deepak referred to class or strata which was so much a part of the Indian social scene.

"Interesting!" Shaku was quiet and thoughtful as she ate her lunch. If Hakim left, her days would be dull. They were both the only children of their parents. Both craved companionship. But for their stations in life, they could have been friends.

Shaku's empty plate was lifted by Mustapha and taken into the kitchen where Amina Bi took it from his hands to wash. There was already a stack of brass and copper vessels. A mountain of charcoal ash lay in a brass 'thaali' or plate. Amina Bi scrubbed with a palm-full of coconut husk. The vessels shone. They were kalaid or silvered every six months by the wandering 'kalai-wallah.' He heated strips of tin and silver and covered the inside of each vessel. Amina Bi knew that when the silver wore off, the unpolished surfaces could cause stomach problems.

Amina Bi shared the kitchen duties with Durgi and Gulabo. Even though Pushpa and Deepak asked her not to, she felt that it was her duty to supervise the kitchen as a form of repayment for all that the Baksh family had done for them.

"Thank Allah we have running water here. Hakim's father," she never spoke his name out of respect for her man, "do you remember fetching water from the stream in Afghanistan? We young ones seemed to be carrying water throughout the day. But we were strong and could run uphill without feeling any fatigue! I still miss the pomegranates and cold wind."

"We shall go back some day Amina, I promise you." Mustapha caressed her covered head affectionately with long, work roughened fingers. He was not sure if he had made another empty vow.

- -

CHAPTER II

"We are not born as the partridge in the wood, or
the ostrich of the desert, to be scattered everywhere;
but we are to be grouped together, and brooded by
love, and reared day by day in that first of temples,
the family"....H.W. Beecher.

A BOY FROM AFGHANISTAN

Mustapha and Amina Bi had served the Baksh family
for as long as sentient memory could recall. For
the Pathan, Khas, on the outskirts of Kandahar was like a
paradisiacal dream scented by almond and apricot blossoms,
coloured with shockingly red, giant pomegranates and
surrounded by mountains covered with thick snow. The
summer brought in fields of poppies in its wake. Giant
pink, red and white ones swayed in the breeze. The farmers
slashed a part of the swollen pod and collected the sticky
white liquid. Opium was one of the most lucrative crops.
The world had still not discovered its hallucinatory potential
and luxurious sense of well being, which made people wildly
rich.

Mustapha and Amina Bi often talked about the cold, clean air, unpolluted streams and tender 'dumba' sheep and goat meat used in biryanis and curries. Mustapha had come to the household as a fifteen year old, left by a Pathan money lender who had been robbed of all his cash as he trudged through Thugee country. The Vaid treated the wounded man with herbal pastes and consoled his frightened but unharmed son. The Pathan was grateful for the Vaid's kindness. He recounted the hazards of his profession and said it was dangerous and not suitable for his child to follow, considering times had worsened and little moral sense was to be found amongst the populace of India. He did not want Mustapha to adopt the same trade. He hoped that the good doctor would teach the lad his profession and employ him as a compounder.

The Pathan had a large family at Khas who tended the poppy fields. Early on in life, he had shown his father that he could handle money well and for the benefit of others. As the boy was adventurous and bold, the father introduced him to the money lending trade. There was always a cash surplus from slabs of raw opium. Lending brought in huge interests and the young boy was capable of a little arm twisting if borrowers failed to repay the loan. As always, India was the right place for rich pickings. The father had not taken into account the Thugees, tribals who lived in the forest and way laid travelers, often killing them if they resisted.

Vendors carrying carpets, pashmina shawls, sun-dried apricots, nuts and precious stones were easy prey for the officially accepted criminal tribe. Life was cheap and a few wandering traders and minstrels lost or rotting in the woods were of no consequence to anyone, least of all the 'Angrez' rulers, who considered them 'collateral damage' in the colonies they ruled. The robbers were only afraid of the British soldiers who seldom ventured into Thugee domain except for shikaar. A tiger or bison's head was worth taking 'home' to Blighty for the boys to see.

Knowing of the worsening law and order situation along his chosen route, the Pathan begged of the Vaid to keep Mustapha. He requested that the good doctor educate the lad so that he could help with his patients. The Vaid agreed but made the mistake of not consulting his wife. The money lender slipped away one night, never to be seen again. Mustapha understood his father's silent, unemotional departure. Afghans were tough and the men never showed any form of weakness.

"He may have gone back to Afghanistan," Hari told his wife when there was no sign of the Pathan.

"He maybe dead!" snapped Rameshwari as she stirred a pot of dal over the wood fire. "And we have been landed with his abandoned, Mussalman son!"

"I'm sure he can help you around the house." Hari's tone was soothing and placatory.

"Over my dead body!" snapped Rameshwari, visibly angry.

- -

Vaid Hari Baksh was very generous and tolerant. His heart went out to the boy left so abruptly in his care. He wished to raise Mustapha as his own son, but Rameshwari would not hear of it.

"He's not even a Hindu! What will my family say? Even his shadow cannot fall on my aged father. The poor old man will have to bathe at least thrice a day, and call pandits for 'shuddhikaran puja,' to wash away that mother of all sins! My Amma's spirit must be already tormented, at this very moment, as you speak. Your Karma must be good, that is why you are married to me. I'm very tolerant and do not object to his presence. He is a human being and we are all made in the same mould. But that's how far I am willing to tolerate him."

"That's kind of you!" Rameshwari did not know whether Hari was paying her a compliment or being sarcastic.

"He can take care of the outside work, watering the plants, sweeping the garden and burning dead leaves. Can he milk the buffaloes? I thought not! The milkman can teach him. I am willing to send his food out to him, but he will get no salary. He can also play with Deepak. Just imagine how tolerant I can be, allowing a boy like him to touch my son! Seems a tough lad... he might be able to give some of that ruggedness to our over sensitive beta! He has changed so much since Pushpa arrived!"

Rameshwari continued her nervously frenzied rearrangement of cushions on the diwan in the sitting room. She straightened out, stood still and wagged a slender finger in her husband's face, "But remember, he is not allowed into the house! I shall cook his food and give it to him outside. He can look after your garden. You do realize he will have to earn his keep?"

"Yes I do," answered Hari, as he led Mustapha to the stables where three buffaloes, two cows and a tonga horse lived in complete and blissful harmony. "You will have to help me build a room for you tomorrow. There are plenty of bricks lying around. Till then can you spend the night here?"

Mustapha touched the Vaid's feet. "I can stay anywhere you want me to, Hazoor. I will repay this great debt. I will do whatever you and the 'Maalkin' tell me to do."

The kindly Vaid put his arms round the boy's shoulders. "You're not a slave! We shall look after you. I am sorry you cannot enter the house. Customs are strange and cruel man made laws to keep people down. They are created to counter human insecurities and fears!"

"Don't worry Hazoor... we are loyal Pathans. You will never regret having me around. Is my Abba coming back? Did he say something to you before he left?"

"He will, I am sure of that. Till then treat me as your father. I shall fetch you a mattress and some blankets."

That night, when Hari went to the stable to check on the boy, he felt the damp pillow and noticed tear streaks on the boy's unwashed cheeks. Looking heavenward with folded hands, he whispered, "God... I don't care whether you are his or mine... do send his father back to him!" But the money lender never returned.

Though he was not allowed to enter the bungalow, Rameshwari looked after Mustapha well. He grew into a strapping young man with the typical, rugged, aquiline features of the North-West Frontier. He often thought of his father and the land they had left behind. He did not recall his mother who had died in child birth.

During one of his trips into town, he bought a pomegranate sapling and planted it outside his brick and cement room. The fruit was stunted as it was not exposed to the bracing, dry climate of Afghanistan. But it comforted Mustapha and acted as a reminder of Khas, his village near Kandahar. When he chewed the tiny pink seeds, he imagined the ruby red fruit of his childhood and swore that he would go back some day.

Mustapha worked hard and the garden flourished. Deepak and he devised every possible game their young minds could think of. Deepak's loud laughter could be heard once again. The Pathan taught his young charge the art of kite flying. They spent hours challenging other colorful paper creations in the sky above. Many exciting moments were spent cutting them down with spools of glass coated thread called 'manja.' Often, when the wind was strong, the string, stiff with glue and crushed glass, sliced their palms. The boys would hold their hands together, allowing the blood to mingle. Then they would lick the blood off and run after the rudderless, floating kite before anyone else could steal it. Their stock never ran out. They climbed trees and chased imaginary enemies with bows and arrows made by the young Mussalman. Out of his mother's earshot, Deepak called his companion 'Bhai,' for that is what he was, in camaraderie, spirit and thought.

For Deepak, Pushpa's presence in the house was necessary but not intrusive. She helped Rameshwari through the daily chores and snuggled up, exhausted, against her boy-husband at night. In an age when child marriage was the norm rather than the exception, sex and passion bloomed at a slower but more natural pace. Companionship was the instinctive reaction of such children. There were times when the young couple would sit down to play marbles on the red and blue Persian carpet in their bed-room. Even Ludo and Chess were welcome distractions in a day dominated by norms and traditions laid down by the elders. To speak out or disagree was not an option. To obey the eldest member in the family was. Nothing warranted an opinion from the juniors, particularly the women. It was not evident if anyone felt stifled by these unwritten laws. From the times of Manu and long before, rules were passed down through song and story. Each festival and season had its own gods, etiquettes and principles. Following them to the letter was a sign of cultural emancipation. Scientific reasoning was not applicable.

Mustapha was dispatched daily to the market to buy fruit and vegetables. It perplexed him to think he could buy and handle food for the Baksh table, but could not touch it in the house, but then this was Hindustan, not Kandahar!

When Pushpa came to live in the bungalow, Hari decided that Mustapha needed a bride too.

The quest for a Muslim bride was daunting. Rameshwari was not in favour of it. "There will be children, more mouths to feed, dirt. How can you think of such a thing?"

"Don't be selfish Wife!" Hari was a mild man but when he grew angry Rameshwari would hold her tongue. "You have only provided him with food and shelter. You have not bought his soul! He has never been given any money to spend. It is time we paid him and set him up as a householder. He must have his own family."

In the end, it was Rameshwari who settled matters. An Afghan carpet vendor arrived at the door. He carried two rolls across his massive shoulders. "Do you have a daughter?" she suddenly broke in, as she picked a small carpet for her husband's office.

The man was startled. "Maalkin, I'm selling you fine, Afghani carpets, not daughters!" He was most indignant.

41

After a while, when Rameshwari paid him for the small rug, he relented. "And no, I don't have daughters, only sons!" he chuckled with satisfaction. "I'll see what can be done."

"Do forgive me! There is a young man here... from your community. He needs a bride... think about it."

The carpet seller returned within the week with a proposal for an acquaintance's daughter. The Baksh's accepted it on Mustapha's behalf. Hari, Rameshwari, Deepak and Pushpa plunged into frenetic preparations and Mustapha was married to Amina Bi. Another simple, brick and mortar room was added to the existing outhouse and the two households settled down once again.

"It was all like a 'khichdi,'" sighed Durgi. "The whole family and the Mussalman's father-in-law, jostled around, were confused and made a mess of every tradition. Finally, when the wedding was over, they settled down like vegetables always do in a khichdi."

Shaku was curious. She wanted to know all about Mustapha's past. She felt he was her key to the son. Through him she would be able to understand Hakim better. The strapping young Muslim attracted her. She recalled his anger when she kicked him in the back. The fire in his eyes was exciting. It was the first time she had caught his attention and been able to make him speak to her.

"Ma, why is Tauji so stern? He seldom smiles and yet Baba calls him 'Bhai'. Why does he serve us instead of sitting with us? Why can he not live in this house? I know he follows a different faith but aren't we all the same? Baba says we are."

Pushpa did not look forward to Shaku's uninhibited chatter. There were questions she could not handle; answers she was afraid to put into words. "Why don't you talk to your father? I don't really know much about Tauji."

When Shaku settled down in Deepak's study, he knew it would be a long afternoon. The very fact that she wanted to know, meant that she was ready for all the drama and horrific details of the past twenty years.

"It's a long story, child. Often a very sad one. Are you prepared to listen to it?"

"Of course I am Baba! I am not a baby anymore."

"No you're not. Your mother was speaking of marriage today. Would you like us to find someone for you?"

"We'll talk about that later. Tell me about Tauji first."

"Do you remember your grandfather at all?" Deepak asked his daughter.

"Hardly! I was only three when he died. What happened to him Baba?"

43

"I think it was a cancer of the small intestines, but he would not go to a hospital. Being a Vaid he tried to cure himself and then it was too late!" Regret and sadness tinged Deepak's words. "He was the kindest, most humane man I ever knew. All that he did for Bhai was risky and dangerous at the time."

"Tell me Baba…" Shaku whispered as she adjusted the cushions under her head and stretched out on the colorful diwan by her father's side. He settled down in his favorite planter's chair, legs astraddle across the broad, spatula like, wooden arms.

- -

"Bhai's wedding went off without a hitch." Deepak told Shaku. "It was a quiet affair conducted with dignity by the Quazi from the mosque. None of the neighbor's came for they weren't invit-ed. Bauji thought it was better so. Your grandmother laid out quite a feast for the young couple, but strangely enough, did not attend the ceremony. She talked about her parents' spirits being in great distress."

"A strange woman, wasn't she?"

"Not strange but very afraid. She was afraid of displeasing her gods; she was afraid of being defiled by an untouchable's shadow; she was afraid your grandfather would bring disaster upon the family through his new fangled ideas. She attributed his illness to every new idea that angered the household gods. She believed that her gods were the only true ones and they had to be worshipped in the ritualistic ways she had been taught by her mother. She believed that all human beings are packaged according to their previous births. Nothing could change that or shift the preordained route of their destiny."

"Then why did she look after Tauji so well? Was he not out of her caste loop?"

"I think she was very fond of him. She felt very sorry for the abandoned child. He was just two years older than I, but nothing would make her accept him in the house, till…" Deepak's voice trailed off as he looked back into those distant days of sorrow and turmoil.

"Till what?" Shaku was impatient.

"I was at the Christian Medical College in Ludhiana, when Bauji collapsed. There was no way I could be informed. Ma called Bhai into the house and together they took him to the railway station by tonga. They brought him to my college but by then it was too late to save him. Bauji lingered on for a month and a half. He was in great pain. Bhai nursed him to the end. Ma never forgot that. When she got back to Jullundur, Bhai, Amina and the child were allowed into the house. Nothing was said, no deals were struck. They just walked in to help with chores in the Bari Kothi."

"So one man's death was the ticket to another's entry into paradise?"

"It was hardly paradise! India was wounded by the Partition. Blood flowed through her streets; fires added to the carnage and stench of death."

"I remember asking Ma about the brown pumpkins that floated under the bridge, over the river Beas, as the train brought us back from Ludhiana. She told me they were just pumpkins, but I knew they were bloated bodies... I just knew."

"I have seen trains full of corpses, as they steamed in from Pakistan. I even treated babies who had somehow survived under the bodies of their slaughtered parents. But thank God, it is all over now!"

"Is it Baba?"

"Yes it is Shaku. Isn't Bhai a living testimony to that change? When the riots broke out, Ma did not let him go to the bazaar. Men were being stripped, their private parts examined to ascertain their faith. The neighbors knew we had a Pathan and his family in the house. They came one night with lighted torches. So many had been burnt alive! Ma stood at the gate with a stick in her hand. Can you imagine? Just a stick! She told the mob that the Mussalman was afraid and had run away. The crowd wanted to come in and see for themselves. Ma let out a string of Punjabi expletives and ran into the crowd brandishing the stick. Many of them had been treated by Bauji. They could not face Ma's wrath. Grumbling, they went away. Bhai,

Bhabi and Hakim were hiding under your bed! If they had discovered them, we would have all been killed."

"And then?" Shaku's eyes were wide with terror. She asked herself what life would have been like without Hakim. He was so much a part of the household, even through his silence.

"A smoldering country simmered down. Bhai and family remained hidden for days. We gave them Hindu names for a few years."

"Really? And what was Hakim called?"

"Harsh, I think!" Deepak and his daughter laughed uproariously. Searing memories melted away into the redundant pages of history.

"Dada was a great man, wasn't he?"

"Yes he was... one of the heroes of my life. Such ordinary people change the course of history."

"What about Dadi?"

"As a child she intimidated me. She seemed so fierce and un-bending. I longed to have Bhai in the house with me. She would not allow it. She always seemed angry with the both of us. Yet, she arranged his wedding. She chased the mob. I realized that Ma had a soft heart enclosed in bones of steel. By the time she passed away, we were very close to each other. There is a lot of her in you."

"I am glad!" Shaku said. "Now that Dadi is gone, why can't Tauji live with us?"

"I have begged of him to do so. But he is an uneducated, simple man. He feels he owes us a great debt which can only be repaid if he serves us. Bhai would be uncomfortable with us and amongst our friends. Nor would our society accept him. I have built more rooms for him and now I plan to put Hakim through college. His report card from the Government School has been outstanding. Have you seen it?"

Shaku shook her head. "He barely talks to me. I find him quite insolent!"

"He is very reserved and shy, but he is a solid young man with great values inherited from wonderful parents."

"Too solid!" agreed Shaku as she got up. "Baba, I have to go to the market for a few things for school. Can I ask Hakim to take me in the rickshaw?"

"Why not? Do tell your mother before you go. She might want to accompany you."

"Ma, are you coming with me?" Shaku asked Pushpa.

"I don't like your going alone, but Hakim is reliable and I have a back ache. Be home for tea."

Shaku took Mustapha's permission and Hakim brought out the cycle rickshaw. The horse driven tonga of Vaid Hari Baksh's time had been replaced. Shaku climbed in and sat on the seat which was covered with a canvas hood against the rain and sun. The hood hid her face, a safety precaution against inquisitive, prying eyes. Though the purdah system had died out, girls were the most shielded members of an Indian family.

- -

"Do you remember the summer of '47?" Mustapha asked.

"Hai Allah! It was dreadful!" Amina Bi shuddered as she thought of the horrors of Partition, the metallic smell of fresh blood, the stench of burning corpses and homes. Amidst this carnage was her husband's trip to to Ludhiana, to be with Huzoor, who was admitted in the American Hospital.

Vaid Hari had tried to cure himself with herb teas and pastes but the pain in his stomach grew more acute. He refused to let Deepak take him in for a check-up. He did not believe in allopathic remedies. When he could not walk or eat, Rameshwari and Mustapha took him by train to Ludhiana. The Mussalman cared for him till the very agonizingly painful end. He still shuddered when he recalled Huzoor's animal like screams when the pain was too much to bear. As the good Vaid's strength ebbed, the noises became subdued moans and finally there was a chilling stillness. Vaid Hari's illness and demise opened the door to the Pathan who was finally accepted in the Baksh household. The depleted family could not do without his and Amina Bi's ministrations.

"He was the kindest man I ever knew... after my father!" he added hastily, duty bound to remember the father who had abandoned him in a strange country.

"I wish I had known your Abba, but it was not to be. Destiny has brought us here and our lives are inextricably entwined with this household. They are good people. How can anyone call them infidels?"

Mustapha held her slender, work calloused hands in his and looked into her eyes. "I shall take you back some day. We will eat the ruby red pomegranates and feast on biryani. We will go back and show our son the land of our forefathers. There is no place on earth like our land."

Amina Bi touched her husband's hennaed beard as tears misted her vision. In her heart she knew she would live and die in this strange land. Afghanistan was not for them in his or her life-time.

- -

CHAPTER III

"The smallest worm will turn, being trodden on;
and doves will peck, in safeguard of their brood."...
Shakespeare.

AN ASSAULT IN THE MARKET

"An all weather, all encompassing hood! It is almost like a purdah or burkha!" thought Shaku with an inward chuckle. At least she could go out in a covered rickshaw without a chaperone. Her mother had not enjoyed such freedom. As Hakim drove slowly and carefully towards the bazaar, Shaku thought of her mother's plight and smiled. The whole scenario had been so out-dated and amusing.

Pushpa was the first girl in the Batra family to get a basic school education. When Deepak married her she was a mere babe in arms. Till she joined him at age twelve, she was sent to the Punjab State Vernacular School, which ensured that she finished the fifth grade, with Punjabi as a compulsory language. A curtained, horse driven tonga took her to school and waited outside the gates till she was ready to go home. Some of her friends hitched a ride. Those moments shared with the girls, cocooned within starched white muslin curtains, were some of Pushpa's happiest childhood memories.

"We laughed a lot and shared a lot of secrets," she told Shaku.

"Did you talk loudly or in whispers?"

"Loudly I think... we giggled all the time! Our stories were pretty explicit in their details."

"But then the tonga-wallah must have heard everything!" Shaku was genuinely shocked.

"Probably... but he was not supposed to listen in. Servants never expressed an opinion or discussed all that happened. If they were indiscreet they were dismissed. If any one of the family paid heed to their stories, petty politics would come to a head and lead to shouting and screaming. Hair pulling too! Family squabbles took a long time to heal. Nothing could be sorted out except through the intervention of the head of the house, my father, your Nanaji."

"Could you move out of the ancestral home and live on your own? I'd hate to live with people I could not get along with."

"Shaku, you'd never be able to cope with the kind of life we had. It was a joint family. It shielded us from the outside world. If one member did not pull in enough, the others looked after him till matters improved. Pitaji made all the financial and executive decisions. His word was law and he was very fair. In my time girls did not get an education but when Pitaji heard your father would go to college, he insisted I went to school too. None of my sisters did."

"Did all the married ones have separate bedrooms and kitchens?"

"We had our own rooms and toilets. If a new member came in, another wing was added to the house. The kitchen was huge and served the entire family. I wouldn't have had it any other way. Working in it was fun as we had great girlie sessions while we prepared the food. Your Dadi was the uncrowned queen of the kitchen. Even I got slapped around a couple of times when I put extra salt in the vegetable curry."

"That's awful!"

"You are spoilt in comparison. I would like you to remember what your grandmother once pointed out. There had been a vitriolic slanging match between the eldest sister-in-law and your father's youngest brother. My sister-in-law wanted to move out of the house to another place. Your Dadi compared us to a sack potatoes. She said every shake would settle the potatoes in the bag. The large ones would settle at the bottom and the smaller ones move to the surface. No one left the house and we all learnt to live together. Each fight settled the potatoes better. We learned to share and give more of ourselves. It was an exercise in maturity."

"I love your quaint stories Ma. Did any men teach at your school?"

"Only our Urdu masterji. We girls sat behind a thick curtain and never saw his face. He did not know when some of us crept away. We took turns in sitting behind the curtain so that he'd think we were all listening. The funniest part was when we flirted outrageously with Maulvi Sahib, and asked him very personal questions about his love life. He ignored us and droned on with the lesson as if he hadn't heard a word. My friend Bilquees once put out a bangled hand from under the purdah and asked him to press it as it hurt due to too much written work, especially with a script that moved in the opposite direction."

"Did he?" Shaku was all agog with curiosity.

"Certainly not, but we could almost see him blush."

Shaku's reverie was interrupted when Hakim stopped in front of Sandip Stationery Mart. His back was towards her as he informed her, "I shall be parked in the shade under that tree. Just call out to me."

Shaku recalled her mother's Urdu teacher and put out her hand. "Aren't you going to help me down?"

Hakim's hand was moist as he extended it towards her. He still did not look her in the eye. Shaku smiled as she put one manicured hand in his and the other, for a brief moment on his shoulder. He almost carried her off the rickshaw. A quick glance revealed the crimson colour that stained his neck and face. "Why does she do it?" Hakim asked himself angrily as he parked the rickshaw under the gnarled old neem tree. "Why does she make it a point to embarrass me?

She is spoilt and cruel! She is always making fun of me and I hate it. The sooner I leave for the American School, the better. She thinks she can have her way all the time. Look at the way she kicked me! I may be a servant but we have feelings too. In any case I did better at school than her." The last thought made him smile.

Hakim bought himself lemonade from the cycle cart nearby. He watched as the thick sugar syrup, salt and crushed ice was mixed in a pan. The ice slabs were stored under several layers of jute bags. When required, a corner of the jute was removed and an ice pick used to break the pieces. The juice of two small limes was squeezed through the fingers of the left hand to separate the seeds. The liquid was then poured from a great height into a very tall glass. This was done at least three times to blend the syrup perfectly and create a fleeting froth. Hakim had never seen a single drop of the precious drink fall to the ground. No surplus water was added and as the ice melted at its own slow pace, the customer took unhurried sips over a long time. Hakim treated himself to a 'nimboo paani' quite often on hot summer days.

His attention was drawn by a ruckus at the grocery shop. A customer wanted a kilogram of un-refined sugar gur, from the lower layers of the open sack. "Too many flies and bees are sitting on top... why can't you keep it covered?" she asked.

"And lose all my customers because they can't see what they are buying? Leave it be Bibiji! Where have you come from... Amreeka?" The man used a red plastic swat to hit the offending insects. They were killed on the slab and the shopkeeper removed them with his fingers.

"You don't have to be so insulting!" the woman fumed. "I will go to another shop. I shall not eat filthy, germ infested stuff!"

"Do that!" spat the shopkeeper. "Be an Indian in Bharat Desh. The Angrez took the germs with him." This parting shot was aimed at her retreating back. The watching, idle crowd laughed in delight. The shopkeeper grinned broadly, pleased at being the centre of attention.

Hakim loved the market. It was disorganized, bustling, colourful. The traders called out to him personally, enticing him to inspect the wares. Saris, salwar kameezes, underwear, flowery padded bras, shorts, trousers, leather belts and briefs hung like colourful banners outside the garment shops. In areas where illiteracy was a norm, goods had to be displayed in their physical form, not through brand names. Garlands of popcorn, rice and wheat puffs were strung in doorways at the snack and grocery stores. Oranges in long, red, net sleeves were wound around pillars at fruit and juice stalls. Red, dried chillies from various areas and of varying potencies lay in bulging sacks and made the passerby sneeze. In a shady corner, under a large banyan tree, cages with pigeons, parakeets, kittens, rabbits and puppies were on display. Most of the bird cages were strung from the hanging roots of the tree. Hakim even spotted a rare pheasant. He knew that the animals and birds were poached or stolen.

Through the corner of his eye he spotted young Memsahib with a package under her arm. He pretended he had not seen her. He was still angry about the kick and very obvious teasing. He knew she would go to the pet cages and argue with the owner about poor living conditions. The shop owner had to make a living and humoured the girl. He bantered with her and promised to improve matters by her next visit.

It was a very hot day. He had lost a cage full of partridges, inadvertently covered with a thick cotton quilt. They lay in various stages of dying. "What are you going to do?" Shaku asked, visibly shaken by the carnage.

"Nothing! Nothing at all! They are worth at least a thousand bucks. Someone can buy them for their table."

"Oh noooo!" wailed Shaku.

"Oh yeeees!" imitated the owner, fed up by the interference of a girl who did not understand the monetary implications of his loss. Then he brightened, and looked towards Hakim. "Unless of course you buy them for dinner. I shall give the lot at half price. They are not quite dead and your Mussalman rickshaw-wallah can wring their necks and clean them. Good idea... eh young Memsahib? You'll help me make up my loss too."

The man did not mean any harm. He was bantering with the girl as usual. "Whaaaat?" screamed Shaku, horrified at the suggestion. Her angry wail brought Hakim rushing to her side.

"What did he do? What did he say? Did he hurt you? What did you say to her?" he asked the man, holding him by the collar and dragging him into an open space, away from the cramped area.

"I did nothing! I didn't even touch her." The frightened man wriggled under Hakim's hands. He was scared out of his wits. A crowd gathered as was their wont in a crowded place where everyone joined in to watch a free tamasha, and give unsolicited advice.

A coolie ferrying huge bags of flour from a parked truck to the grocer's shop, threw his sack down and came towards Hakim. The fight was a welcome diversion from the tedium of his work. He caught hold of the boy's shirt tail and pulled, ripping the seam to the arm. "Oye!" he shouted. "Are you trying to be a filmy hero? Which one? Shashi or Shammi?" He swung at Hakim's nose and threw him to the ground.

The shopkeeper who had been whimpering all this time, suddenly found his voice. "Maaro, sale ko maro! Beat him, beat him! He is trying to impress young Memsahib... Sala Mussalman! Cursed Muslim! Says I hurt her! Do you believe him?"

Shaku saw that matters were getting out of hand. She was afraid Hakim would get beaten by the crowd which was getting restive and were flailing their arms and shouting in support of the shop owner. The word "mussalman" was bandied around. She caught hold of Hakim's hand and dragged him towards the rickshaw. The mob did not try to stop them as a woman was involved and the police invariably took cognizance of this fact. Shaku climbed into the rickshaw and Hakim pedaled fast, weaving through the traffic at breakneck speed.

By the time they got home, Shaku had lost all her new found courage and cried hysterically, unable to explain what had occurred. Pushpa gave her a warm cup of milk and Deepak insisted she had a Valium to put her to sleep.

Hakim stood in the middle of the sitting room and explained to his parents and the Baksh's the trivial incident that led to so much pandemonium.

- -

CHAPTER IV

"That courage is poorly housed which dwells in numbers. The lion never counts the herd that is about him, nor weighs how many flocks he has to scatter."... Hill.

THE FAMILY

Amina Bi's tears were scalding as they flowed into the chai she prepared for Pushpa, who did not say much but cried into her sari pallu. The two women huddled together on the string charpoy, the warmth and sweat of their bodies forming a barrier against a confusing often hostile world.

"Hakim protected my daughter, like the brother she never had!"

"Bhabi, your daughter saved my son's life! How can I ever repay that debt? You and your family have protected us for so long... Allah will always be with you. Your father-in-law, Vaid Hari started a tradition of tolerance that generations to come will follow. Our lives have been inter-twined with yours. Our very existence has been ensured by your family. But your country does not want us... where do we go; who are our people? We are outsiders, firangees, foreigners, Mussalmans! We have no country, no home..." Amina's unsaid words bracketed the grim truth of the day.

Pushpa had no answers to give, only tears and the warm circle of her arms.

Mustapha walked with Deepak through the orange trees. "I want to go back to Afghanistan. That is my home, my family will be loved and respected there." He held Deepak's hands in both his as he made the announcement.

"Bhai! After so many years, who will know or remember you in Kandahar? They knew your father but you left too early to make a mark. Hakim would be completely lost. How will you pick up the threads of a life so long gone? The Russians have taken over your country, it would not be safe for you to go back. I am here with you, and swear before God I'd give my life if anyone touched you or your family."

"Don't I know that? We are putting you in danger too by staying here. Your love for me and mine is like an impending threat, an invitation to foreseeable evil. Man is the worst of God's creations. He is cruel for pleasure, not merely to satisfy any needs."

"Bhai your vision is blurred by sorrow and anger. You are mistaken in your reading of one incident that cannot be generalized." There was firmness and conviction in Deepak's voice. "My country is as tolerant as it is vast. Its people follow a hundred different cultures because they are descended from a hundred different races. That in itself proves how tolerant a people we are. It's people often suffer minor convulsions but heal them-selves again and again. More often than not goodness prevails. We are a hospitable, friendly people who live and let others live too."

"If Shaku had not pulled Hakim away, he would have been badly beaten, even killed. It has happened before!" Mustapha's questioning eyes were dark with horror. "My little brother, I helped you pull out those half burnt children from that orphanage They did not stand a chance against the marauders! You stitched the men with sliced off penises, mutilated ears and noses. We both comforted terrified women and girls who had been raped again and again just because they were of a different faith. Men laughed and took turns as they defiled them. How can you of all people preach tolerance and friendship?"

"Those were moments of madness, retaliation for what happened across the border. This country ought not to have been torn apart, but the Angrez always left divisions in his wake. Some of our leaders took advantage of the rift and asked for a partitioning of the land. We are still paying for it today! Read about the border skirmishes and you will realize that a cohesive, bonded people ought not to have been forcibly compartmentalized. We are a single brotherhood and should never have been ghettoed into separate nations under the banner of religion."

"You are an idealist, little brother! I am a simple Pathan, not even a Pakistani, but your people club me with them! There are good people across the border too, but why are all Mussalmans viewed with suspicion?" Mustapha's voice shook with anger.

Deepak hugged him. "Exactly what I feel! You and I are so alike that I am amazed! My people are your people too. You and I are blood brothers! Do you remember the time I cut my finger on glass coated thread during a kite fight? You solemnly picked up a discarded blade and incised your finger too. We held our wounded tips together, letting our blood mingle. Bhai, if you go away, I shall be like an amputee. Can you live with that?"

"I cannot see my family harmed... I love them too much."

Deepak's eyes blazed with anger "You forget that they are my family too! You choose to live separately but only a weak, brick wall stands between our homes and hearts."

"What can I do?" Mustapha shook his head in despair. "Amina and I are so confused and frightened!"

"Bhai, please stay! We love you. Haven't you experienced that ever since you walked into our lives as a child? Whatever happened today was an aberration, a mere ripple. These malignancies come up sometimes, not only in my country but all over the world. Kandahar will be no better. I beg of you to stay. Think of Hakim's future. He is bright, ambitious, focused. He wants to better himself. Can Kandahar do that for him?"

It was the thought of Hakim's future and his love for Deepak that persuaded Mustapha to change his mind. As he sipped chai with his wife, he explained to her the pros and cons of living on in his adopted country.

Amina Bi was not convinced. "Do you remember how we hid from the mob? They would have butchered us if they had found us in the house. Do you not recall the families murdered even though they were promised safe passage to Pakistan? I can never forget the bloated corpses thrown into the river like so much carrion... the bleached skulls kicked around by children! Crows, hundreds of them, like a black cloud, feasting on human flesh! How do you know it'll not happen again?"

"How do you know this will not happen to us in Afghanistan?" countered her husband. "Would we be safe in a country where bullets fly as we try to get rid of the invader... where tribal war lords try their best to annihilate their so called enemies, families and all, leaving no trace of life or its outer trap-pings? I can promise you nothing Amina. I can give you no assurances but I do have faith that Allah is watching over us and will not let us be harmed unless it is His will. My little brother is right when he warns of an uncertain future, if we go back. Here we live under a protective umbrella provided by this well known family. Remember it was Bari Memsahib who staved off the mob.

Hakim will be well educated at the American School. Maybe someday he will move to the USA and we can join him there."

"We shall always be refugees and second class citizens here!" Amina was despondent.

"In Soviet Afghanistan we shall be worse than refugees... we will be prisoners with few options or choices! We are Pathans, a proud and independent people. I do not want my son to be cowed down by anyone. Hindustan offers him a chance to move on. It is a free country, un-oppressive, extending equal chances to those who merit them. He will be the one to fulfill our dreams." Mustapha did not realize how prophetic his words were.

Amina Bi could not fight against her husband's resolve. But she longed to see her own family who occasionally sent letters through wandering carpet vendors. "I wonder how Abba and... Ammi are? Are my brother and sister still alive? I am afraid for my people in Kandahar...we have had no message from them in a long, long time!" Amina Bi clung to Mustapha as a fresh wave of gut-wrenching sobs convulsed her body.

"Our land will be free some day. My people would rather die than be ruled by outsiders. I swear that someday I shall take you back to your loved ones and the pomegranate trees." Mustapha held his wife in his arms, in a rare display of affection. "Come! Let us take a walk in the garden. Hakim is at the well... let us put his mind to rest. Words and work will help all of us get over this ugly incident."

- -

At first Hakim was quiet. He was afraid his parents would blame him for the fracas.

"You did well my son... I am proud of you!" said Mustapha, chucking him under the chin.

"Abba I ran! No Pathan runs from the field, and that too dragged off by a woman!"

"You did the best thing possible. Can you imagine what our plight would be if anything happened to you? We would not be able to face ourselves!" Amina Bi touched his face as she consoled him.

"It is an uneven playing field in the city! Never attempt anything foolish my son. But why did you assume the man had harmed Shaku?" Mustapha had wanted to ask his son the question since his return from the market.

"She was upset seeing the writhing partridges and I am sure that man said something unpleasant to her. I'll thrash him when I meet him next but it will be without young Memsahib!"

"You will do nothing of the sort!" his father admonished him. "The matter is over, forgotten! You will not go into that street again and that is an order."

Hakim looked down at his feet so that his father could not gauge the expression on his face. Some day, when he got a chance, he would avenge his humiliation.

- -

Pushpa ran gentle fingers through Shaku's hair. The girl stirred and then turned over to go back to sleep again. "Should I let her be?"

Deepak shook his head. "If she does not wake up now her sleep cycle will be disturbed for the next two days. She'd better have some food too."

Irritable but awake, Shaku was told to have a cold bath and then come down to dinner.

The meal was over, the kitchen cleared. Shaku had not spoken a word throughout the evening. She had told them nothing of what had occurred in the bazaar. Deepak and Pushpa bade their time and waited for her to say something. The girl was strangely quiet and very calm. Within the ambit of a single day she seemed to have matured into a young woman. Pushpa was anxious. She missed the constant chatter and unending questions. Was the girl in shock? She had been hysterical when she came home.

"Is something worrying you my sweetheart? Baba can always put it right... you have only to ask." Deepak was as worried as Pushpa and resorted to the third person as he had done when Shaku was a baby.

"I am alright Baba, Ma. I am not frightened any more. My mind is very clear now. You might misunderstand me, but whatever happened in the bazaar today, has opened my eyes to the reality of India at this moment."

Pushpa shuddered. She had never before heard her daughter talk so solemnly. She had to be unhinged and distraught. Deepak heard a woman speaking. She appeared confident and capable. He was proud of her but a little apprehensive too.

"Baba, Ma, I have always loved you and never lied to you. I have been stupid and often talked too much and taken advantage of being an only child. You have given me whatever I wanted. My joy has ensured your happiness. Isn't that so?"

"Of course my baby girl... but why the long face?" Deepak asked as he tweaked a strand of her hair.

Shaku looked her parents full in the face. "I want to marry Hakim."

Her directness took their breath away! There was a stunned silence. Deepak got up and started pacing around the room. He always did so when he was tense. Pushpa stuffed the sari palloo into her mouth to stop a scream. Tears spilled over, along her nose as she looked around the room with wide, staring eyes, looking for an escape from the dreadful nightmare unfolding before her eyes.

Palpable tension filled the usually cheerful room. "Why?" asked Deepak. Silence shattered like tiny pieces of glass. "What made you take this sudden decision? Does he want it too? Have you two discussed all this?"

"Baba we have hardly exchanged two words let alone discussed this! I think I've always liked and admired him.

68

The mob in the market made me realize that he is the one I feel safe with... he will never harm me or ignore me. He respects me. I can feel it in my bones."

"That is not enough reason for marriage!" Deepak dismissed his daughter's plea with an impatient wave of the hand. "You feel safe with me too! This is just an impulsive, spur of the moment decision. I will not agree to it!"

"You cannot marry a Mussalman!" The words were stammered out by Pushpa.

"And why not? Give me one good reason. Did all your talk about equality and oneness mean nothing?" Shaku demanded.

"I meant every word..." said Pushpa "but has today's incident taught you nothing? You will always be talked about, pointed at and even be in danger from people who do not accept inter-caste marriages."

"Hakim and I can face them!" said Shaku with determination.

"You are too young! So is Hakim. Has he been leading you on? I shall kill him with my bare hands!" Deepak was furious and not his usual calm, collected self.

"Baba, he won't even look at me! He has kept his distance and place, whatever that may mean! He has never spoken to me, because he accepts his postion as a servant."

"I will not allow this! What will the family say?" Pushpa anticipated insurmountable barriers, a lot of snide remarks and non-acceptance from the community.

"He isn't working; his parents will be most uncomfortable with our family... what are you asking for child? This is one wish I cannot fulfill for you!" Deepak was beside himself with despair.

"Sit down... the both of you." Shaku was authoritative and very defiant. "Listen very carefully to me. You have known Hakim from the day he was born. He has no rotten habits and is studying well. You said he was focused and bright, which means that given the right openings he will do well in life. After the American School he can get a higher degree in some college. He is capable of it. There will be lucrative jobs to follow. He is healthy and strong. We will have sturdy children. He looks after his parents well. He has been brought up on little, so will never hanker for more. We know and love his parents. Taiji will never be unkind to me. Tauji already treats me like his daughter. Do I have to say anything more about the qualities of a good groom? In fact he is a made-to-order-husband."

Deepak was astounded by his daughter's arguments. Whatever she said was true. "You are both too young!" he repeated weakly. "Who will feed and clothe you?" Deepak asked.

"Who did that for the both of you when you married each other as babes in arms? You and Tauji will have to do the same for us. We shall marry when we both can start earning. Till then we shall get to know each other better. He thinks I'm a spoilt brat!" Shaku laughed.

"Keeping you in mind, I have met the mothers of so many suitable boys…" Pushpa's voice trailed off as she saw all her dreams of a grand Punjabi wedding falling in a heap around her feet.

"Ma your suitable boys have horrible fire eating mothers who rule their sons and daughters-in-law with an iron rod! Do you remember Ritika? She married Arjun. His mother is a dear friend of yours. He earns well and shares a grand house with his parents. But Mataji interferes in everything! She tells Ritika how to sit, stand, eat and dress. She even objects to Arjun spending time with his wife! On the other hand, Taiji will make a wonderful, understanding mother-in-law."

Pushpa was surprised. "I didn't realize Anjana was so harsh! She seemed such a nice person. What if Hakim does not want to marry you?"

"I think he will have no objection. Ma, I'm a woman too. A woman's instincts are never wrong! Tauji might not agree at first but you can persuade him Baba, can't you, for your baby girl's sake?" Shaku looked appealingly at her father.

Deepak's heart melted. "You will make an excellent lawyer! Maybe that's the line you ought to pursue in college. We shall talk to Bhai and Bhabi tomorrow. And if they do not agree young lady, you will have to make do with someone of your mother's choice!" He wagged an admonishing but playful finger in her face.

Pushpa looked at her husband as if he was a lunatic. "Are you going to agree to this idiotic scheme of hers?" Then she left the room in case she said too much.

- -

"What a fine woman our child is turning into!" Deepak commented as Pushpa and he lay in bed and tried hard to come to terms with a life-changing day.

"I told you she ought not to bathe in the garden!" hissed Pushpa. "You allowed her too much liberty and now we are landed with this willful, strange demand!"

Deepak turned on his side and rested his head on an elbow to look at his wife. "Whatever she said is reasonable and true. We know Hakim well. He has no major faults. He is quiet and hard working and I will help him through my contacts. He will look after her as she ought to be. And they shall always be living near us."

"So we will go through this farce some day? Are you not going to dissuade her?"

"Certainly not! My daughter's happiness comes first."

"But he is a Mussalman!" Pushpa wailed. "How will we face our relatives, our community?"

"He is also a fine young man. If our friends and relatives cannot perceive that, then they can go their own, separate ways. Tomorrow morning you and I are taking our daughter's proposal to Bhai and Bhabi." He was determined not to listen to his wife's almost hysterical protests.

For Deepak, often principles became reality and he saw himself as a crusader who could change situations that had gone revoltingly wrong. The Hindu-Muslim divide, was, to his mind un-natural. These were two communities who had lived in peace for centuries. If he could lay a single brick to build a new foundation, he would do so. Pushpa called his ideas "Grandiose schemes without any substance or reality. He lives with his head in the clouds!" she told a friend. Deepak hoped to go down in a small space of local history "as a man who did the right thing." Vaid Hari Baksh was remembered as such. The son had no greater aspirations. He wanted to "die a decent man." There were a lot of unanswered questions; many hurdles to be overcome; much planning to be done. For the sake of his child's happiness, he was willing to take on the world.

After a while Deepak groped for his wife's breast. He traced his fingers around the firm roundedness, the petal soft, velvety skin that felt warm to the touch. She pushed his hand away, hurt, confused at the different signals that emanated from him. Deepak smiled in the dark. Tomorrow would be a brighter day. Pushpa would soon come round to his way of thinking. Shaku would be radiant.

It had been a long day. Deepak was sure his father, Vaid Hari Baksh, wherever his spirit was, was proud of him. About his mother Rameshwari's reaction, he was not so sure.

CHAPTER V

"Who loves the rain and loves his home, and looks on life with quiet eyes, him will I follow through the storm and at his hearth-fire keep me warm."— Frances Shaw.

AGAINST ALL ODDS

B hai and Bhabi could not comprehend what was being said. Their son and young Memsahib? Mustapha's first thought was that the willful girl from the Bari Kothi had made overtures towards his innocent son, who was now being blamed and coerced into a farcical relationship as a cover up for all misdoings. As of this moment, like Amina Bi he was determined to go away for the sake of family honour, but he would thrash his boy within an inch of his life, to make him understand the gravity of the situation. Honour lay foremost in Mustapha's mind.

It took hours and many cups of tea to convince Bhai and Bhabi that this was not a cruel joke but the decision of a girl who was mature, educated and brave. Deepak talked to Hakim in the presence of his parents.

"My son, do you think you could accept my very strong-headed daughter as your wife?" Deepak asked with a smile. Hakim said nothing but acknowledged the fact with a slight inclination of the head.

"Speak to Huzoor!" Mustapha commanded. "We have been honoured by a great family."

"I shall defend young Memsahib with my life," was the quiet, sure reply.

That night, the Muslim family gave thanks to Allah for the recognition and kindness He had bestowed upon them. In all their years in the Baksh's service, they had never hoped for more than an employee's due. Their nostalgic longings for Kandahar, the gigantic mountains and icy plains of Afghanistan, were unfulfilled dreams, a part of an unknown destiny which had no beginning or end. This defining moment with Deepak and Pushpa, was a culmination of great love and respect nurtured over many years, through two generations of tolerance and humane values.

"We have been accepted, my faithful wife! We will become a part of the Baksh family." There was wonder tinged with disbelief in Mustapha's voice.

"This is a single family that is accepting us," was Amina Bi's cynical response. "I am afraid of the future."

"You do not know when to count your blessings!" Mustapha ticked her off.

The arrangement was kept secret from the Baksh and Batra families. Frenetic activity started as the two room tenement, originally built by Vaid Hari Baksh, mushroomed into a modest but well designed annexe. The neighbourhood accepted the fact that a faithful servant was paid for his selfless service. On the face of it, nothing changed. Amina Bi insisted on washing utensils while Mustapha did the odd chores, but Bhai and Bhabi were now referred to teasingly as "Samdhis" or in-laws.

Shaku made a concerted effort to chip away Hakim's stoic reserve and silence. She began by asking for his school reports. His marks were far better than hers. He pointed this out with pride. She acknowledged the fact with grace but assured him that some day she would be far ahead. Hakim already knew that she was a woman of substance and unflinching courage. She would bear him strong children. The day he left for the American School, Shaku held his hand for the first time. He squeezed it and said, "I'll be home for the weekends."

"I know. I shall wait for you."

- -

"Young Memsahib has taken a shine to the Mussalman!" said Gulabo to her mother. "I feel it in my bones. They never talk to each other, but are always exchanging sly glances. I can see a storm brewing... a lot of unexpected fun!"

"Stop your idle chatter and get on with your work." Durgi tacitly agreed with her daughter's observation. "I wonder if the Maalik and Maalkin know? They would never encourage such a relationship. I have seen the Maalkin meeting prospective sons-in-law. They will have to pay a huge dowry for any one of them. They can afford it too."

Gulabo, who seldom spoke to Shaku, except to receive orders about ironing and mending clothes, tacking on buttons and helping wash the young mistress' long hair, could not resist saying, "She will marry the man of her choice while Ramu is lined up for me! I do not want to live with that wimp."

Durgi slapped her daughter hard across the mouth. Red welts appeared on the child's cheek. Durgi's voice was harsh, menacing but defeated. "Never, never say that again! You know what lies in store for you if you do not accept that proposal?"

Gulabo wiped the tears from her eyes and the spittle from her mouth. She opted for the second option rather than the first.

- -

On a wintery night, a brick crashed through the bedroom window at the Bari Kothi. The glass pane shattered. Pushpa clung to Deepak in fear. By the time he wrapped himself in a shawl and went out, the miscreants had disappeared. He reported the matter to the thanedar, the head policeman in charge of the local police station. The man offered him a cup of tea, wrote a dairy report and promised the matter would be looked into. Not even the police dared to ignore Dr.Deepak Baksh, one of the best physicians in Jullundur. Even the all powerful police department needed to go to a doctor and a little 'bhaibandhi' or brotherliness always paid off.

"Do you have any enemies Sir?" the thanedar asked.

"Not that I know of."

"Could be friends of the Mussalman who lives in your home. You never can tell with these people. We keep a constant eye on them. Can't be trusted."

Deepak was furious but wanted to avoid a confrontation. "I trust Mustapha and his son with my life. Please do leave them out of this conversation."

"We shall do our best Doctor Sahib, but you never can tell, especially when you have a young daughter." Did he detect a sneer in the man's tone?

Deepak realized that his own servants had been gossiping. He knew nothing would be done as the police were biased against Muslims. The Partition had honed elephantine memories into hatred and it could take generations to erase the seething mistrust, emotional hurt and word-of-mouth horror stories of massacres on both sides of the border. Hakim and Shaku would have to be even more careful than usual.

At a time when telephones were a rarity and would-be clients had to await their turn for a governmental allotment, Shaku looked forward to the weekends to see Hakim. When there were exams or internships he would be away for over a month and the long period of separation was difficult for both to bear. Even when he came home, to maintain an atmosphere of normalcy, both talked in whispers, away from prying eyes. This meant that Hakim still worked outdoors at the well and in the garden and conversation was possible only at night, before they went to their rooms. Never again did Hakim drive Shaku into town. Amina Bi was made to stop washing the Baksh's utensils, a job taken over completely by Durgi and Gulabo. Hira, the rickshaw puller sold his shabby, beaten down vehicle to a nephew and plied the Baksh rickshaw with great pride. Deepak bought a second hand Volkswagen from an expat. The tonga and rickshaw were kept more for sentimental reasons rather than their utility. Eventually the old horse died peacefully, instesd of being sold to a tannery for the price of his skin.

Shaku opted to teach young children. In the early sixties, there were very few job options for women. India was just emerging from centuries of reticence and 'purdah.' In the Punjab, where womens facial features carried the genes of beauty garnered over centuries of invasions and invaders, young girls were kept behind closed doors, away from the predatory eyes of rapacious maharajahs and noblemen. A few small rulers boasted of a virgin in their bed, every night of the year. Such a boast carried not only the veiled threat of dominance but also high-lighted the ruler's own manly prowess. The girls were often picked up from villages or off the roads. Parents who accepted a ruler as god-cum-master, seldom protested and often gladly accepted remuneration if they were financially strapped for cash. The British rulers changed this attitude to a great extent by the time they quit India.

But freedom was slow and came at a price. The phrase 'eve-teasing' was created, to define a social malaise which over the years brought its own legal remedies. Soon eve-teasing ranged from a vulgar remark to rape and physical molestation. Caste and conservatism, created their own limits, leading to clandestine sex and perverse attitudes. For a woman, marriage was the first option as it afforded an umbrella of safety. If she wished to work for the economic freedom it ensured, teaching at an all girls school was considered the safest.

If he had a son, Deepak would have insisted he joined his practice. For her own safety and mental growth he agreed to Shaku's pursuit of a degree in education. He even bought her a cycle to go to college, but when some boys surrounded her, pulled the veil off her head and laughed as she lay on the road with a grazed elbow, he asked Hira to drive her in the rickshaw instead.

Travelling by rickshaw did not seem to deter the eve-teasers. One morning, Shaku's thoughts of Hakim were broken as a hand touched her knee. When she looked from under the hood of the rickshaw, she spotted nobody, but at her feet lay a thick, white envelope. Curiosity got the better of her. She opened it to find a well drawn picture of her talking to a sardar, with the blurb, "I love your pink cheeks! I would love to hold your head in the nook of my manly arm." She laughed off the weak English and the incident with her parents, but Deepak warned Hira to be vigilant. A week later the same boy slipped another picture with a blurb that said, "I love you and want to meet you under the flowering trees of Leisure Valley Park." Obviously he accepted her silence as acquiescence.

Hira stopped the rickshaw and looked around to no result. Ten days went by when another fat envelope was pushed in. This time Hira caught the boy, but he was a short haired man, who swore his sardar friend had put him up to the prank for a tenner. Hira slapped him a bit and a crowd gathered to peer at the girl who was the cause of the romance. Shaku was very upset, but not hysterical. She hated being in the limelight.

The next morning, Deepak drove to the Doaba College for Men, and met the Principal. The culprit was found but not punished as the kind doctor knew how hard it was to reverse a derogatory remark from a hard earned character certificate. Besides he realized that young hormones had to find outlets and their vessels needed to be treated with gentleness and understanding. The sardar and his friend came to the Bari Kothi to apologize and the chapter lay closed, except when Shaku and her friends would meet to re-live and laugh over childhood memories. Years later, she asked Deepak for the three illustrations and letters the sardar had written. "Why would you want those?" he asked, surprised.

"Just as a morale booster and to see if the young artist has made it good in the art world."

"I left them with Principal Bhag Singh on the understanding that he would destroy them. I could not afford to have my daughter become an object of ridicule and gossip."

- -

At the end of the two year training, Hakim won the prestigious Carpenter Trophy for Excellence. He knew all that was possible about agriculture and farming, and the American implements that went with it. Deepak quietly and without any fuss, transferred twenty acres of his wheat fields into the boy's name. As they were just beyond the boundary wall of the bungalow, Hakim's working them raised no undue suspicion or speculation in Hira's family.

However, the preferential treatment towards the Muslim, brought on jealousy and snide remarks.

"Now that is a boy I would like as my husband!" Gulabo exclaimed to Khamo, her younger sister, as she watched

Hakim plough the fields, driving by on a tractor. They were looking over the compound wall at the fields that bordered the Bari Kothi.

"He has never even looked at you!" scoffed Khamo.

"He shall for I am prettier than young Memsahib. I have green eyes and a fairer skin. Some day he shall be mine."

"Don't bet on it... he has eyes only for her. And don't ever forget that our father is not yours. You are the 'haramzaadi,' the bastard girl."

Durgi was making rotis when she heard her younger daughter's screams from the servant lines. She rushed across to find Gulabo sitting on the girl's stomach, pulling her hair and slapping her face. She separated the two, beat each for good measure, but could not get an answer when she asked what led to the fight. Even Hira could not elicit a reply despite a variety of threats.

The wedding was planned for November. That was when summer came to an end, the days became cool and nights pleasant. In a country where life is dominated by extreme weather conditions, temperatures play a significant role in any important event. After a summer wedding, newly -weds rush into the comparative cool of the hills. In a rare display of feelings, couples hold hands, cuddle and kiss, secure in the anonymity a new town offers. Young

Punjabi brides are identified by the red and white chooras, bangles they wear from wrist to elbow, right through the first year of marriage.

"There will be no dowry given," said Deepak with mock severity.

"None will be accepted," laughed Mustapha.

"It is up to Hakim to make the farm flourish. We shall have a quiet havan in the house, followed by registration at the court, before a magistrate."

"Is it wise to hold any ceremony in the Bari Kothi?" asked Amina Bi. "The servant lines will be abuzz."

"Bhabi has a point," agreed Pushpa.

"We cannot hide this alliance. I am proud of it and will not cater to public opinion any more. A son is coming into my family. It is cause for celebration, not mourning. We shall keep it low key but not secret. We have done nothing to be ashamed of."

A pall of gloom descended over the extended Baksh and Batra families when they received the invitations.

"There is no question of allowing this to go through," fumed Ravi Baksh. I always knew my cousin was wayward and not fit to head the family. I shall go to my lawyer."

"He might advise us how to keep the property within the family." Prabha, his wife suggested.

"I always knew Deepak and Pushpa were inconsiderate. They refused to stay in this home even when we invited them to. Now this abominable marriage to a Muslim! They have blackened our faces. You must do something about it," the wife urged. "I wonder how the Batras feel?"

A similar vitiated atmosphere plagued the Batra household. As Pushpa and a dowry had been exchanged during Deepak's nuptials, they had none but ritualistic rights over his wife. Collectively they decided to offer no gifts and to keep away from the celebrations. For good measure they sent a letter to Pushpa, ordering her never to darken any of their doorsteps ever again.

Pushpa read the missive and burst into tears. Deepak put his arms around her shoulders. "Does it matter my love? Our daughter is happy. We have gained a wonderful son. Our thinking is correct. We are contributing our bit towards a better world. Why should a few disgruntled relatives matter?"

"Bhai, we ought to cancel the wedding." Mustapha ventured. "I see a hard road ahead. Perhaps Shaku needs to find a Hindu husband."

Deepak spoke softly. "She will think of no one but Hakim. At first it was I alone. Now you are with me and so are our immediate families. We are strong and will conquer all opposition. You must promise that you will see this through and always be by my side."

Mustapha put his right hand over his heart. Words could not express the depth of that silent vow.

Hate mail from relatives and anonymous letters from the community spilled over from the mail box. Shaku read the pages with a perverse delight, laughing uproariously over strange threats in bad English and abusive Hindi. Hakim became thoughtful and followed his fiancee' like a shadow. He would not let her be harmed. Eventually it was decided to travel to Bangalore, where no one knew or cared about the Baksh or Mustapha families. On an un-disclosed date, before a taciturn, disapproving magistrate who sported three white sandal paste lines on his wide brow, Shakuntala Baksh and Hakim Mustapha, were joined in matrimony. To avoid any confrontation, they caught a bus in to Kashmir and spent a month on a house-boat called Taj Mahal, moored by the side of the Dal Lake.

They trekked through the gold and red autumnal trees. It was an idyllic beginning. The people were friendly and polite. The house-boat owner asked a lot of questions. Hakim felt at home amongst the largely Muslim community. Little did the young couple know that their names and addresses were noted carefully in a well worn copy book, kept hidden in a metal biscuit tin, under the floorboards, beneath the dining table in the house-boat.

Mushrooming, disgruntled, dissatisfied splinter groups were noting down names of people who were likely to serve the Cause later on.

- -

"Why have we been given sweets and clothes?" Gulabo questioned her mother.

"Young Memsahib and the Mussalman are married but we are to keep quiet about it," said Durgi.

That night Gulabo let hot tears soak her pillow. Yet another one of her dreams lay shattered like broken glass bangles.

- -

CHAPTER VI

"Oh beware of jealousy; it is the green-eyed monster, which doth mock the meat it feeds on."—Shakespeare.

BURN OUT

Hakim was puzzled by the trampled young wheat. There were no signs of hooves or cow dung pointing towards cattle left surreptitiously overnight in the fields to graze. Nor were there any cropped heads. And yet almost half an acre of tender, green plants were ruined. He was worried and brought the subject up at the evening meal.

"I'm sure it must have been a pack of street dogs. They love the grass to romp in," said Deepak. "The town moves ever nearer as farmers sell out to realtors. Dogs are a necessary evil of urbanization."

"Do you think it could be someone deliberately trying to destroy the crop?" Mustapha asked. His lined but classically sculptured face reflected worry and concern. Years of experience had taught him to look for reasons, to go behind the scenes, to seek motives. Being a Pathan in North

India after Partition, had exposed him to a new learning which was sometimes unpleasant but necessary for survival.

"We have no enemies," countered Deepak.

"Religion is our enemy and poverty the vehicle it rides on. Both are used as a tools again and again to frighten people and lead them towards violence. When poverty is rampant and there are too many mouths to feed, religion fills the belly, roused by politicians who step in to count their votes. Empty bellies create disinterested rebels and game changers! But it leads to crime and conflict and a help yourself situation where starving youth take what they think is owed to them. Little Brother, have you not asked yourself why crime rates are spiraling?"

"I think you do not give enough credence to the tolerance of the Indian people. We are the most hospitable society in the world. Nobody can deny that. We have given jobs to the Nepalese on the tea estates of Assam and West Bengal. Every fifth watchman and domestic servant in North India is a Gurkha. Every Nepali cook who makes 'Indian Chinese' food is a self evolved master chef! We have allowed the Dalai Lama to create his own township in Dharamsala. We have welcomed the Bangla Deshis with open arms. Compare this to the UK, USA, France, Germany and a host of other countries, where people are given visas only when more workers are required and that cruel euphemism 'outsourcing' is used to justify cheaper labour, more unethical practices." Deepak was agitated.

"But you are also an amalgam of different races. The very tolerance that brought us here and made us join the various life streams, has become a weapon to beat us with. We are now the outsiders, seeking jobs and places which supposedly belong to true Indians! I have heard that though the Angrez is unwelcoming, his rules change and evolve according to the times and are fair to all. Indians go by inherited biases and word of mouth stories. Maybe literacy for all might change this, but when?"

The use of differentiating words like "you, us, outsiders," was not lost on anyone and made the little group uncomfortable.

They were all seated on the carpet in Bhai's home. The meal was usually prepared by Amina Bi, while Shaku was out teaching at the slum school, in Janta Colony, Naya Gaon. In-spite of lucrative job offers, she had opted for the Basti school on a meager salary. Shaku, like Deepak wanted to build numerous bridges in a very unequal world. She felt that education was the one way to narrow an ever widening gap. It was a decision accepted reluctantly by both sets of parents. Hakim was the only one who supported her completely.

In deference to their Muslim 'samdhis,' the Baksh's ate from 'thaalis,' using their finger tips. Pushpa served a second round, using her clean left hand. Fresh food was never touched with the eating hand lest germs were passed on. Those that were considered uncouth habits by the

Westerners, had a scientific and plausible reason. It was a delicate, sophisticated operation with its own rules and expectations. Shaku and Hakim used their hands deftly, seated side by side. Occasionally they fed each other choice tidbits as is the wont of young lovers.

Pushpa made a triangular morsel of meat and roti and popped it into her mouth. Licking her fingers clean, she offered a solution. "Let's keep watch at night. We can take turns and look over the compound wall."

"I shall keep watch and Shaku will be by my side." Hakim smiled at his wife. "After all it is our land, isn't it?"

"Of course it is and we shall fight for it! I have a suspicion it is someone who knows our habits well."

That night the young couple sat crouched in the dark shadows of the boundary wall and waited. Nothing happened. They could hear Gulabo, Khamo and the rest of Hira and Durgi's family laughing in the servant lines and felt vaguely uncomfortable, wondering if they were making fools of themselves. For another two nights there were no results. The fields lay silent and undisturbed. Shaku suggested they perch themselves on the tallest guava tree, concealed from the servant lines. In the early hours of the morning they saw three figures, covered in sheets, move into a distant area of the field. With long bamboos the intruders silently and swiftly thrashed the young stalks into the ground.

Hakim scaled the wall and raced to catch one of them. It was Gulabo. The other two escaped.

"But why?" asked a bewildered Deepak. "After all that we have done for you, why would your children do this to us?" Durgi and Hira stood with their hands folded, looking at the ground, in the required posture of humility and weakness. Neither would meet the employer's eye, as was the custom amongst the lower castes or those of a lesser working status. Looking at their downcast faces, Deepak realized that this was the form followed by all animals. Shut eyes or the downward gaze to show submission. Why had he never thought of it before? Are we any better than the animals we compare ourselves to when decrying anyone's lack of sophistication?

"Sahib, don't call in the police. They will beat us and break our bones," whimpered Hira.

"I shall if you do not answer me! Your children have ruined a good part of our crop for no reason at all. Why should I not report the matter to the authorities?" Deepak shouted in anger.

Durgi, who, till then had stood, head down, looked towards Pushpa and spat out angry words, "What have you done for us? We have served you for fifteen years. You have given us left-over food, old clothes and two rooms to live in, that is all! We fetch water from the well. We use the fields to defecate. We have no fans in summer or heaters in winter."

Pushpa was speechless. Amina Bi said, "How can you talk to the Maalkin like that?"

"You keep out of this you 'bartanwaali!' Look at the airs and graces you are putting on. You've washed utensils here for years, just like me. If the Maalik had educated my daughter she could have married someone like your son. But he favoured your child, so shut your pouting mouth! What have we been given? Are we not servants too? But for our wretched destiny we would be where you are today."

"Durgi you do not understand Bhai and Bhabi's status in this house. Ours is an association that goes a long way and which you do not need to know of or discuss." Deepak's tone was placating as he tried to talk to the cook woman.

"I only know that the boy is not of your caste and yet you married your daughter to him. These people are servants like us and you have favoured them. My children are hurt. They have done this in anger and I can understand their actions."

Hira did not utter a word. He was afraid of losing his only livelihood, the precious rickshaw.

Pushpa, who had recovered, cried, her eyes blazing, "Pack up your belongings and leave immediately! I will not tolerate you in my home for another moment. There is no place for disloyal servants like you."

"She is right," said Deepak. "And take the rickshaw. That is my compensation to you, for the fifteen years you have put in. But if I even see you near my property again, I shall call the police."

"Fifteen years of back breaking, filthy work and they still call us disloyal! What have you lot been? Did you ever recognize our services?" With a toss of her head, Durgi stalked out of the house as Hira trailed behind her, unable to say whatever he did want to say. He was grateful for his bread and butter, the rickshaw, and words could endanger its transfer.

"An unfortunate turn of events," said Deepak.

"This is just the beginning!" whispered Amina Bi.

"Quiet wife!" snapped Mustapha. "You have such negative thoughts. Hakim and I shall work the farm together. Three women in the house are enough to carry on the chores. Life does not begin and end with the Durgi's and Gulabo's of this world. If we listened to their ravings and ranting, our lives would come to a standstill."

The matter ended but to avoid further damage, Deepak hired two watchmen for the night. Hameed was recommended by Mustapha and Ashok was the brother of Rakesh, Deepak's compounder at the clinic. The wheat grew to its full height. The kernels were fat and clean. Hakim was satisfied with the profit he made at the grain market.

- -

Durgi and Gulabo's departure from the Bari Kothi created a void in many ways. The two women's constant presence in the kitchen and around the house had been a comfort. Amina Bi and Pushpa divided the chores between them. When Shaku came home, she made the chapattis, heated and served the food. Amina Bi was very careful with the china used for meals. Vaid Hari Baksh had bought the Royal Doulton dinner set from an Englishman who went back "home." It had delicate pictures of a milkmaid in a flowered apron standing amidst cows on a typical English farm. Durgi boasted of the set to friends, and treated it with utmost care. When she left, it became a liability. It was brought out for guests and thereafter stacked on the pantry shelves, covered with white muslin pieces, against the ever present dust. No one but Amina Bi would wash it. Eventually stainless steel 'thaalis,' 'degchis' and air craft metal woks, which were much easier to clean and unbreakable, made their entry into the Baksh kitchen. The shop keeper assured Pushpa that the 'karahis' were not made of metal scrap from planes that had crashed in the nascent Indian Air Force.

"Then why is it called aircraft metal?" asked Amina Bi.

"Behenji, sister, there is scrap left over when making air craft. This is made from that, and that is why it cleans faster! It will last even after you die."

"Durgi never broke or chipped a single piece," said Amina Bi with wonder in her voice, as she washed and dried the plates and placed them on the cemented shelves in the pantry.

"Then why didn't anyone of us notice or praise her? Why did we take all this for granted? Maybe Bhabi, she had reason to be angry," reflected Pushpa.

Amina Bi lit the charcoal fires for the day. Deepak decided that modern equipment was required to save time and tedium. He took Mustapha along to buy four kerosene oil stoves with cotton wicks. The very tedious job of cutting and threading wicks was left to the men. Occasionally, while cooking biryani and delicate meat curries, Amina Bi favoured charcoal fires for the smoky aroma they lent to the preparations.

"Food tastes so different now!" Deepak made the understatement of the day when a dish of 'gobi-mattar' tasted of kerosene smoke. This led to another foray into the market to buy a pressure cooker. The old brass and copper vessels were sold to the kabaadi-wallah by weight.

"You mean you got only Rs. 209 for that stack of bartans that came in my dowry?" Pushpa queried her husband.

"That's it! I am sorry, but the man said they would have to melt all down to make anything useful."

Every morning, various ragmen, with huge sacks slung across their bicycle carriers, started shouting for cardboard, news papers, tins and bottles, outside the Baksh and Mustapha households. Pushpa and Amina Bi loved arguing with them, trying always to earn an extra rupee from the detritus of their homes.

The Indian rag-pickers and ragmen are the scavengers of the community. They are laughed at, treated with contempt and often hounded by the police on suspicion of theft. They have to produce letters from homes that are throwing out stuff, to confirm it is not stolen. They are also the only people who help a household get rid of unwanted stuff that is never used but hard to throw away. They actually pay cash in exchange!

Sonu, the families favourite kabaadi-wallah, wore a red cap, obviously retrieved from household garbage. He had a jaunty walk, was handsome and tall, and visited the neighbourhood daily, giving the long drawn out, familiar cry that identified his trade. "Paypaah, botel, loha, raadi-wallah!" he would shout as he went by.

Sonu was the proud owner of a second hand cycle rickshaw that pulled a large box with high plywood walls. The box was compartmentalized into four sections. Paper went into one; bottles into another and the last two sections were for metals and old clothes. Everything was weighed and paid for. Rarely, when a woman threw out a tattered sari, with gold or silver embroidery, he would present it to the jeweler. The man would burn and sieve it for a small residue of the precious metals. Sometimes he would take the same saris, but in better condition, to boutiques. Their beautiful borders were used for bags, file covers and table-mats, that found a ready market in many countries abroad.

It was a well known fact that Sonu's weights were hollow, so that he could gain more through the extra poundage. If and when his clients had more stuff than he could cart away, Sonu would draw out four bamboo poles from under the box and strips of rough jute cloth. The poles were tied to the four corners of the container and enclosed by jute lengths to heighten the walls.

Pushpa laughed with delight as she saw Sonu improvise the height for a greater load. "You are incredible! Have you ever been to school?"

The boy lifted his hand to his cap, "I am following my father's trade. What would I do with an education?"

"With schooling you would qualify for a Government job," chipped in Amina Bi.

"Are you sure Mataji? People are starving today and cannot feed their children. I have plenty of food for my family and clothes to cover them. Most households give me left-over food. If you see my nephews and nieces, you'll realize how healthy and strong they are" He pointed towards the garbage and said with pride, "This is worth almost Rs.200. Each old tyre and tube will fetch me five rupees. Would the Government give me as much?"

"And what about marriage? When you do get a bride, will your children follow the same profession?" asked Pushpa.

"That day is a long way off. The girl I chose has gone home. I shall bring her back."

With that nugget shared between two elderly women, Sonu walked and pulled the cart along, as the day's pickings were too heavy to be cycled away.

"I think he was referring to Gulabo. I often saw her talking to him," observed Pushpa.

"Could be. She has lovely green eyes," agreed Amina Bi.

- -

Durgi and Hira found another house not far from the Bari Kothi. The terms of service were different and quite harsh. Durgi would cook and clean utensils; Gulabo would wash the toilets and iron clothes; Hira would drive the occupants in his rickshaw whenever required, all free of cost; Khamo would have to sweep leaves from the garden; Ruby and Ravi were to take out the cows to graze in the fields and were to sweep and wash the cowshed. The entire family would get Rs. 200 for all the work done. Jobs were bartered for the quarters, free water and electricity. A hired milkman came morning and evening to milk the cows and buy the surplus for his sweet shop.

"I have never cleaned toilets!" Gulabo protested to Durgi. "We are not untouchables and do not do these jobs."

"We are just one rung above the Harijans, which does not mean much. You will have to do this kind of work here or they will throw us out. I shall look around for another place. How are we going to keep body and soul together on

Rs. 200? If you had not damaged the wheat we would still be with the Maalik and Maalkin. How are we going to fit into one room? Did you children think of that before acting so stupidly?"

Durgi was beside herself with worry and frustration. She had acted boldly, spoken out her thoughts and walked out in anger. She also realized she had left no doors open to re-enter the Baksh household. Hira often returned after a day's work with just ten or fifteen rupees. Sometimes he'd complain his turn did not come at the allotted rickshaw stand. Too many people were buying cars. The tonga and rickshaw were becoming redundant and antiquated. Durgi realized she would have to find ways and means to feed her family. As Hira lay down beside her and fumbled with the tape of her salwar, she pushed him aside and whispered, "We cannot create any more mouths to feed. Besides in this one room the children can see and hear us."

Gulabo and Khamo giggled. They had heard every whispered word.

- -

Durgi's departure was a boon for Lakhi the sweepress and her husband Lallu. Relegated to one corner of the servant lines due to their Harijan status, they had grown old serving the Baksh household. Brought in during the last days of Vaid Hari Baksh, these 'people of God,' named so by Mahatma Gandhi aka 'Bapu,' lived on the periphery, rejected even by Durgi and her large brood. Their task was to creep into the toilets, thrice a day to remove night soil from the commodes. They dumped this into a deep pit in one corner of the wheat field. That scented jasmine and red desi roses grew along the pit was no accident. The shrubbery flourished on rotting feces and countered the stink.

The couple was not allowed into the house for fear of their polluting shadows and presence. Their very being was invisible, their voice silent. Through generations, they had become used to this way of life. In a land where trades were passed on from father to son and mother to daughter in an effort to retain earnings within a family, the 'safaai-wallah,' though a necessity, was considered one of God's lesser, more-to-be-forgotten creations. That they dealt with human waste made them untouchable. Again, the fear of their carrying disease was the scientific reason for their exclusion. Those of their caste, who survived disease and death in infancy, became sturdy people in adulthood. The ironic truth was that immunity was forced on them via their trade.

The caste system in its earliest form, was the most economically sound and safe method of retaining familial wealth based on an inherited trade or occupation. When it started intruding into progress brought on by education, travel and jobs, and an ever increasing population, clashes based on caste became common and murderous. The state failed to create laws to equalize the various castes and to this day, Indians fight for a place in the sun based on breed, groups, categories, quotas and nomenclatures that allow them governmental benefits and subsidies. Modern day India juggles to erase caste groups, but the harder she tries, the more the castes stick together for sheer class identity and the group's physical and economic safety.

For the first time in his life, Lallu stood in the sitting room on the blue-red carpet. He left his shoes outside.

"Can you call Lakhi in too?" Pushpa asked with a smile.

"Will you both be able to clean the two houses in addition to the toilets? Your salaries will be tripled," Amina Bi laid out the terms of service.

"We have never entered the house Maalkin!" said Lakhi with awe as she looked at the shelves stacked with bric-a-brac collected from various parts of the globe.

"Well, you are free to do so now, but leave your shoes outside. The Maalik will have flushes installed within the month and we shall fill the pit outside. Your work will be easier. Lakhi you have to do the dusting too. Bhabi will explain how it is done. Be sure not to break anything," explained Pushpa.

Nothing was mentioned about Durgi and Hira, whose departure had led to elevation in status for a lowly safaai-wallah and his wife.

The old couple touched Pushpa and Amina Bi's feet. Later, as they sat in their sooty room, smiling, eating the previous day's dry chapattis' with smashed raw onions and green chilies, by the light of a smoking tin and wick lamp, Lallu said, "Perhaps, when the time is right, we can ask for one of Durgi's rooms."

"Why would we do that? I am used to this quarter."

"Perhaps!" Lallu repeated as he gazed into the future.

In years to come Lallu's dreams would come true. Long after his death, the Indian people elected Dalit presidents, prime ministers, chief ministers and members of parliament, more as lip service towards equality rather than an acceptance of the same concept. It is a small but significant start; a defining moment that has tried to eradicate a stain so dark that it can never be completely washed away. Present day Indian society will still not permit blood groups to mingle but stresses on caste and gotra, to the exclusion of any other reason or justification. Vigilante groups in villages ensure the purity of blood by killing young people who choose to marry in spite of community warnings. They will hunt them to the end and murder them with unheard of brutality as police men look on, silently and tacitly accepting the indelible mark of each ones birth and destiny. The 'Khap' or village judges run parallel, kangaroo courts, and no elected government in Delhi can be bold enough to stop them. 'Honour killings' follow Indians abroad when children do not follow norms set by the community or the parent country.

"The day will come..." Lallu left the sentence unfinished.

"When?" his wife asked.

"Someday. We are but a moment in the story of this universe. What has happened today is a sign of hope. The human mind will progress beyond these trivialities. After all every human being's blood is as red as ours and his shit as smelly! So where lies the difference?"

- -

CHAPTER VII

"The rules of a slum are written in blood and sometimes with invisible ink."... Commando.

THE SLUM

As Shaku entered the Pre-Nursery, Vidya rushed forward to hug her. She wrapped her stick like arms round 'Maa'm's' knees. The child was too young to speak much and yet, through a few words and a lot of gestures, she made herself clear. With blonde hair, a sign of severe malnourishment, the girl looked younger than her three years. Large black eyes protruded alarmingly from a thin, oval face. "Seb le ayee?" she asked Shaku, who delved into her bag and handed an apple over. Vidya rushed back to her seat and hid the fruit from the other children, saving it for "tiffin-time." She would never share even a sliver of the precious eatable.

Shaku badgered Vidya's parents at every PTA, and insisted that a meal had to be provided. After two months of constant pleading with no visible results, she decided to bring something from the Bari Kothi for the infant. The gesture was against all rules as the child then appeared to be her favourite. The mother, who cooked fresh food for fourteen people residing in three rooms at the slum, said that Vidya being the youngest and a girl-child at that, was served last. Often there was no food left for the mother or child.

"Vidya still drinks my milk," she said with pride."She will not sleep till I suckle her."

"You cannot be having any milk!" Shaku was shocked.

"Of course I do... that is why she sleeps so soundly!" The mother smiled, confident of her own, starving body's capability.

Shaku realized that Vidya went to bed hungry every night and decided to seek the help of a health promoter, from the government dispensary, to explain dietary requirements to the parents.

The pile of toys was distributed. Vijay, who had shown violent behaviour at play time, was handed a doll with yellow hair. An hour's 'role play' was fixed for the day. "Do you have brothers and sisters?" Shaku enquired.

"I have a behen... she is just born and I do not like!" Vijay spoke in staccato pigeon English.

"Take this doll. She is your sister... look after her." Shaku hoped to calm the child. The moment her back was towards him, Vijay pulled the doll's limbs and hair apart and handed the torso back, saying, "Toot gayee... it is broken!"

Shaku was appalled. Did Vijay hate his baby sister so much or had he seen some violent, sexual behaviour at home? At the PTA, the father came across as articulate and confident. The mother hardly spoke but smiled a lot. Shaku's gentle prodding elicited no answers. People from the slum were very secretive, afraid of any repercussions. They felt that shared confidences were leaked and led to further violence and unpleasantness. The health promoter, who visited Vidya's hutment, observed that being the youngest daughter-in-law, the mother was overworked. The other 'bahus' helped by fits and starts while the men gambled over cards during their free time. Some worked, while others lived off others. The umbrella afforded by a joint-family, brought security as well as starvation where a large number of people were involved. The food chain too was dependent on the pecking order. The eldest member got the pick of any dish, whatever his or her age. Vidya's grandfather was a huge corpulent man. His rotis were smeared with 'desi ghee' or clarified butter. He asked for water from the daughters-in-law and children whenever he felt thirsty. He would not even tie his own shoe laces. As a retired government employee and head of the family, he was least concerned about what the rest of the family ate or whether it was enough. In his eyes it was payback time.

The Health Promoter who visited Vijay's home had a different story to tell. Ram Dulari, Vijay's 'mother,' worked in five homes, cleaning utensils and doing the sweeping and swabbing. Dharam Singh was a peon at a government office. He had opted for a government job instead of at his father's illicit distillery, the moment he realized that his younger brother Commando was the chosen head of the family. He came home in the evenings well after dusk and long after his wife returned. He usurped her salary as his right, being a male and her husband, but bought clothes and footwear for her at Diwali. She was never asked her style or colour preferences and was grateful for a generous husband. In return Dharam expected hot, fresh food in his 'thaali' by the evening. When Ram Dulari's younger sister came from the village, in the hope of earning something towards a lean dowry, Dharam started sleeping with both women. He considered this his right, as he fed and clothed her and allowed her to bank her salary. Vijay's "sister" was the result of this illicit union. To save face, not a word was spoken and the family and neighbourhood maintained a discreet silence.

The slum rules dictated everyone lived like a family. Each one helped the other in times of need. A few favours in return were acceptable. Shaku realized that her moral values could not face the test of a poverty stricken colony. Another student was Daljit, whose hut was a long shed with a tin roof. It froze in winter and could fry an egg in summer. As farm lands were sold and bonded labour "freed", hungry relatives reached Daljit's home to share food and opportunity with those who had already hit the imaginary jackpot. No one was turned away but the food became scarce and infants and women suffered. Daljit was a happy child. He studied well and came first in every exam. Shaku realized that the only way out of the slum was education. The world would offer many opportunities to Daljit, if he did not succumb to the slum first.

Shaku's pragmatic approach made her see that the slum rules were quite different to hers. They had nothing to do with human rights or the Constitution of India which she had learnt verbatim from her school books. She could not condemn these rules or change them but she could try to understand them. They were a living organism, changing according to the needs of people. But, they were followed and for that very reason a slum, which had open drains, no toilets, one room tenements, no potable water and very little food, survived. Its people obeyed the rules. Discipline was often strict and brutal but it worked. She started reading books on Child Psychology as a way to help Vijay cope with a chaotic life.

"Vijay!" admonished Shaku. "What are you doing?" The little boy pushed aside his classmates to grab the green and red plastic slide. He refused to stand in a queue or let the others play. He kicked and tugged, slapped and bit to get his own way.

"I am Commando! He comes to my house. I kick and beat people like he does."

"And who is Commando? Do I know him?"

"He is my Chacha. Can I bring him to school?"

"Of course you can." Shaku did not give the matter a second thought. But she liked the idea that someone who understood her destructive protégé, would be interested enough to visit her.

Monday saw Vijay walk into class late. He swaggered as he entered holding the hand of a dark, stocky youngster just past his teens.

Pride made Vijay's eyes gleam. "This is my 'chacha,' Commando," he told his classmates. "He will beat you if you do not listen to me."

"Oye, little nephew, what are you saying?" the swarthy youngster asked. He turned to Shaku, "Sorry Madamji!"

Shaku looked up from her register and asked, "Are you really his uncle?"

"Yes Madam. I am his chacha. His father's youngest brother."

"And is your name Commando?"

"Most of the colony calls me that."

"Why?"

"For no reason at all." The young man shrugged his shoulders.

Hoping to motivate and understand Vijay more, Shaku asked Commando to visit the school whenever he found time. He was very muscular and obviously did weights. A silver chain, a jade neck-lace and a pendant with Shiva's head adorned his neck. He also sang at a three star hotel and was willing to contribute to the school children's' birthday parties. His left hand sported four silver rings with different stones. As he later explained to Shaku, the moon stone was to curb his anger; the pearl to bring peace; the coral to increase his virility and he'd forgotten the purpose of the green jade. On his right hand he sported a gold ring embedded with tiny diamonds and a copper one with the likeness of Shirdhi Baba. His long hair was left loose in winter and tied in summer. He wore a scarlet scarf around his neck and old fashioned bell bottomed jeans. The little finger of his right hand had a long nail painted red. Commando said it was to clean his ears. A bracelet of wooden beads encircled his left wrist. His right hand sported the largest watch Shaku had ever seen. The total effect was bizarre but charismatic. Shaku understood why he was a hero in Vijay's eyes. Commando was too colourful and macho to ignore.

One day Shaku's rickshaw failed to report at the school. Commando was on hand and offered to drop her home in his van. Grateful for the help, Shaku accepted the offer.

"Are you married?" Shaku asked the obvious question put to all Indians of any sex.

"Not yet. I shall be by the end of this year."

"Have your parents someone in mind?"

"I have decided to marry for love. That seems the best way," said Commando as if it was a superior way of life he was opting for.

"Do you have someone in mind?"

"A girl who studied with me in school. I have known her for eight years. My parents have agreed to let us marry."

"And how old are you?"

"Twenty. She is a year younger."

"Will you invite me to your marriage?"

"Of course I will."

"However," persisted Shaku, "all marriages are the same in the end. You have to make them work."

Commando glanced at her as if she was stupid. "Madamji, this way I get to choose my bride, not someone who is pock marked and as fat as a cow. And my parents have agreed to a love marriage. It is the best."

"But Commando, in the end marriages are all the same, whether it be for love or an arranged one. You have to work hard on them to make them successful and happy. Marriage and parent-hood, are the most difficult, yet least recognized jobs on earth. Obviously you are basing your ideas on films not reality."

The boy was silent. He did not think it was worth trying to convince a woman who could not tell the difference between the two kinds. In his eyes the rich and educated went in for love marriages, whereas uneducated, poor people from the slum opted for the most lucrative proposition. Though barely educated, he was earning enough to choose the former option, which would glamorize him in the eyes of the Basti.

Whether it was his uncle Commando's presence or Shaku's frequent praise, Vijay's concentration and behaviour improved.

"Ram Dulari and Vidya's mother are the true heroines of our times," said Shaku as she helped Amina Bi lay out the food.

"Who are they?"

"Just women from the Basti. They are self sacrificing and courageous." Shaku went on to tell her mother-in-law about Vijay, Daljit and little Vidya.

Commando walked in one morning at tiffin time, ostensibly to discuss his nephew's future. "Can I talk to you for a minute Madamji?" He was not his usual, confident self.

Shaku took him to the store room where they sat on broken, yet-to-be-repaired chairs.

"Tell me."

"They are not allowing me to see her."

"Who are you talking about?"

"The girl I am to marry! Have you already forgotten about my love marriage even after I invited you?" he sounded peeved, and was obviously not used to being forgotten, whatever the reason.

Shaku listened as he poured out his grief. Deepu's parents were arranging a boy for their daughter. She had told them she wanted to marry Commando but they were adamant. He was not of their caste. That was reason enough to look for another boy. They locked her in a bedroom and would not let her see him. They were torturing her, particularly her brothers, who used cigarettes to burn her arms.

"Are friends allowed to meet her?" Shaku asked.

"Just one," he answered.

"Ask her to bring a signed statement from Deepu to say that she is being coerced into marriage against her will. As she is an adult, we can go to a women's group for advice."

"I shall lay down my life for her but will not let another man take her." Commando declared, a little of the old swagger back in his stride.

Shaku consulted Hakim who said she ought not to embroil herself in a controversy of this nature. Shaku could not understand her husband's attitude considering what they had undergone for each other. She contacted various organizations and handed the telephone numbers to Commando. He visited a lawyers group that meted out free counseling. A month later, Shaku took him aside and asked if matters had been sorted out.

"Yes Madamji." He smiled. "I found out she was already married to the same boy. She had lied to me. I have been saved from a bad alliance. My parents are looking out for a beautiful girl for me."

Shaku shook her head in disbelief. Was love so fickle that it ended an eight year relationship within a month? Or was Commando up to omething which he had not told her about.

Soon after, the decomposed body of a young girl was found in the forest outside the Model Town. The police could not identify her as the face was disfigured, smashed with a brick. There were no missing women from the area, reported in their files. The killer had absconded. Shaku spoke to Commando. His expression gave away nothing.

"The rules of a slum are written in blood and sometimes with invisible ink. Obviously the girl, whoever she was, did not follow the rules."

Shaku shuddered and asked herself if the parents, husband or lover had meted out their own form of brutal justice. She did not tell her family of the incident. They would not have allowed her to work at the Basti.

CHAPTER VIII

"Poverty is the wicked man's tempter, the good man's perdition, the proud man's curse, the melancholy man's halter."... Bulwer.

POVERTY'S PRISONER

Durgi's husband Hira coughed out phlegm laced with blood. His chest was painful and he did not have enough energy to ply the rickshaw. Durgi served dal and rotis at every meal. The family received equal portions of whatever was cooked. The Mehta's did hand out leftovers but these were few and far between as they were an old couple who ate little. Gulabo, Khamo and Ruby worked as part time cleaners, washing dishes, sweeping and swabbing the floors in any homes where they could find jobs, but the money was never enough. When Hira went to Dr. Gupta in the market place, the man asked for Rs. 150 as consultation fees and prescribed a load of medicines, which could not be bought as there was no cash. In desperation, he went to Deepak Baksh's clinic. The doctor looked up but did not recognize his former employee.

"Yes? What can I do for you?"

Hira fell at his feet. "Maalik, do you not recognize me? I am Hira. I am dying. Please do something for me."

Deepak was shocked to see the condition of the rickshaw puller. He was emaciated, white haired and old beyond his years. He immediately called his assistant and ordered a battery of tests which confirmed his worst fears. Hira had Tuberculosis of the lungs.

"You will have to take expensive medicines. I shall buy them for you. But you will have to eat fruit, vegetables and meat. A good diet and the medicines will put you right."

"When will I get better? I cannot drive the rickshaw any more. We have no money for the kind of diet you prescribe."

"You have to rest a lot. The treatment will last for nine months and will be administered by the government dispensary, free of charge. Come and see me every month for a check-up," said Deepak, handing Hira a hundred rupee note. "Buy yourself some wholesome food and don't share it with the family."

For the first time in many months, Hira looked cheerful as he entered his quarter at the Mehta's bungalow. He pulled out the crisp hundred rupee note and showed it to Durgi. "I should have gone to the Maalik a long time ago. Your stupid pride kept me away."

Durgi's nostrils flared in anger, but she made no comment. In her eyes the colour of money did not change whichever the hand that doled it out. Gulabo returned after a hard day's work and flopped down on the straw 'chattai' mat that lay on the floor. "Give me food Ma. The work is killing me!"

"Get it yourself!" shrieked her mother. "One would think I've sat at home all day."

"Bapu, what have you got? Did you ply the rickshaw today?"

Hira told his step-daughter about his visit to the Baksh clinic. The next day when he opened the cloth bag for the hundred rupee note, to buy some fruit, he found none. A frantic search yielded nothing. Gulabo came home with huge danglers in her ears. "Who gave you those?" asked Durgi.

"The Bibi on Mango Lane."

Gulabo did not know what hit her when Hira picked up a thick branch, stacked in the corner as cooking fuel, and swung it across her head. She fainted. Durgi threw water on her face. When she came to, she heard Hira screaming, pointing towards her earrings, "The haramzaadi used my money for those! How will I get well again?" There was utter despair in his voice.

It was hard work extracting the name of the jeweler from Gulabo. Durgi went to the market and got back Rs.50 as the tradesman said the earrings had become "second hand goods." Hira tied the cloth bag to his waist and felt the comfort of the heavy coins against his bare skin.

"So what if I am a bastard child? I am the prettiest around this area. I will do something to get me out of this hell hole." Gulabo was determined to find her place in the sun.

"You are beautiful! No doubt about that," said Durgi. "If you play your cards right we can make some money off you. I have never worried about you. You will find someone." She looked at Khamo and Ruby, who sat on their haunches, listening to the exchange of words. They grimaced and poked their tongues out at Gulabo, from behind Durgi's back.

"I am worried about them. They look like their father. Who will want them?"

"Khamo can have Ramu. He will suit her; she has no spirit at all," said Gulabo, showing a rare burst of sibling generosity.

"Yes! Yes!" agreed their mother testily. "Maamu has another son who will do for Ruby. But what can we do with you, my lovely filly? You are proving a handful, just like I was." There was a nostalgic wistfulness in Durgi's tone.

Lala Bharat Kumar owned the largest and best sweet shop in town. He seldom ate at home as he found the 'kulcha-cholas' from the shop far more exciting. He found his wife's cooking insipid, tasteless and 'healthy.' He always articulated the word with a sneer. He found his wife insipid too. As a result he had bloated into a rotund man with a gleaming skin and three bag-like chins, which enveloped a couple of thick gold chains. The Lala's sex life had come to a standstill, thanks to his corpulence. Munni Bai, his wife was reed thin, with a face like a dried up mango. She seldom smiled. She was a dutiful woman, who looked after the house and crept around on silent feet, head covered, eyes to the floor, as was expected of her. However, inwardly she seethed with righteous indignation and had a wasp's tongue which every one feared, especially her husband and children. The only luxury she allowed herself, was a maid to clean the utensils and sweep and swab the floors. Munni Bai, who was proud of doing all the work as a dutiful housewife should, could no longer bend as much as before. She had always used a feathery broom and had never heard of a vacuum cleaner. The 'jharoo' broom raised more dust than it expended. When Gulabo came into her life, she allowed herself the luxury of visiting old friends and her family.

Gulabo did her work quietly. She did not want to give Munni Bai a chance to complain or get rid of her. Lalaji puffed up the stairs and let himself into the apartment above the sweet shop. He was feeling heavy and uncomfortable after a plateful of potato samosas and felt the urge to take a short nap. "Where is the Laalan?" he asked the girl who was sweeping out the bedroom.

Gulabo looked up and said, "She went down to buy something from the 'pansari'... the local grocer."

"Funny," thought Lalaji. "I never noticed her before. She is beautiful and has green eyes!" Something long-forgotten stirred in his loins. Her dupatta lay across a chair and he saw the cleavage between two young breasts. Panting he reached out and cupped the two globes through the neck of her shirt.

Gulabo did not protest. She had been waiting for such an opportunity, as it worked out to be a bonus, added to her salary. It offered freedom from a prospective and hateful marriage to Ramu, and as an opening into the markets, where she could buy the clothes and ornaments she so craved for. When it was all over, Lalaji gave her a crisp, new hundred rupee note. Then he removed one of his gold chains and handed it to her, saying, "This is in return for your virginity. I have never tasted anything so sweet!"

Gulabo knew that her latest profession would allow her to indulge in luxuries she had never dreamt of. Her mother had tutored her well. When the sweet maker whispered, "Will you come again tomorrow?"

"I am your servant Lalaji... I am always here."

Gulabo and Lalaji's liaison was no secret. Durgi had tacitly prepared her bastard child for a way out of their grinding poverty. Munni Bai visited the shops downstairs whenever Gulabo came to work, leaving the apartment free for the flagitious relationship. Her feelings towards her husband were non-existent. Over the years they had died through his constant sneering, sarcasm and uncouth habits. Gulabo's ministrations made him easier to handle. Many of her friends approved of such an arrangement in their lives as it bought them a perverse kind of freedom.

Gulabo handed her stepfather a hundred rupees. He returned fifty, but she insisted he kept it. "You are a good man Bapu. We will look after you and make you well enough to ply your rickshaw."

Hira, a little recovered over the past few weeks of good food and medicine, put the money into the cloth bag around his waist. He touched Gulabo's head and whispered, "God bless you my child." It was the first time he did not regret the presence of the 'haraamzadi.' When Durgi returned from work, she saw the gleam in her first born's eyes. She knew her suggestive tutoring had borne fruit. She could now get on with the work of settling the other three children.

"Ravi!" she called her son. "Get some laddus from the market... the best saffron ones. We have to celebrate."

"Celebrate what?"

"Gulabo has a new, well paid job."

With a silent nod of her head, Durgi gestured to her daughter to come out onto the road. As they walked, she asked, "Did you wash yourself?"

"Of course I did!"

"Next time, use the phenyl you scrub floors with. We do not want any babies."

Gulabo laughed. "That man is so fat he would not be able to produce anything but samosas. He is like those plastic dolls... all stomach with a tiny head on top. You bought one for me, years ago. It swayed from side to side due to its incredibly huge, rounded middle."

"You never can tell. You have done well. We will have enough food now. Give me the money. You can keep ten rupees and buy yourself some clothes." As she handed over a modest wad of notes, the girl did not mention the gold chain she had hidden in a bag, sewn into her salwar. She was smart, she was beautiful. The combination would take her places.

- -

Ravi's Geography teacher cuffed him on the ear. "You are so clever at Math... what happens when you study Geography?"

"Madamji, I have never seen the world. How can I know about it?"

"Read, read and read more! The world will be yours through words." Ravi thought the woman was off her head. How could mere words show him the globe?

In an apology for a staff room, Santosh discussed Ravi with Shaku. The Nursery teacher was now Principal of the Basti School. "He is bright and street smart. But for a Class II student, he is remarkably illiterate."

"Maybe I can be of some help. Remember Vijay? He is growing up well. Let me talk to Ravi." When he came to the staff room next morning, Shaku realized Ravi was Durgi and Hira's son, but did not reveal her own identity. Ravi was an infant when she last saw him.

"Do you have any problems my child? Do you bring a tiffin everyday?"

"Yes Madamji."

"How are your parents? Do they attend the PTA? I have not seen them here." Shaku had a sneaking suspicion that they did not come because she was Principal of the school.

"They work very hard and have no time. I shall grow up like my father and earn a lot of money," declared Ravi. "My sister Gulabo brings me sweets from the Lala's shop. She even buys clothes for everyone."

Shaku, who remembered Gulabo well, sighed, almost sure of how the money was earned. "You can do much better than your father. Work hard and you shall earn well. Come to me during the break and I shall help you with Geography and English."

Slowly but surely, guided by some unknown power, Durgi and her family started renewing their contacts with the Baksh family. It was as if their destinies were interlocked and nothing could keep them apart.

- -

When Durgi found Gulabo vomiting food in the open drain, her worst fears were confirmed. "Did you use phenyl each and every time?"

"The bottle was empty and the Laalan did not buy more till later."

"How long ago was this?"

"About a month …."

"You could have told me! We must get rid of the child before it is too late. Let me talk to Ravi's father."

That night Durgi and Hira came to the conclusion that Gulabo's condition could be a boon. They decided to talk to Munni Bai to open a blackmailer's front for more cash.

"He raped our daughter. He must pay for it!" Durgi beat her chest and wailed loudly in Lalaji's kitchen. "We shall go to the police if we are not compensated. Gulabo's life is ruined!" Lala Bharat Ram, locked in the store room by his wife, heard every word.

Munni Bai picked up the broom and started raining blows on Durgi and Hira's heads. She pushed them out of the house, whispering menacingly, "Go! Go to the police, now! I know how your daughter enticed a good man. I also know that she stole his gold chain. We shall see who the police will listen to. Get out and never let your daughter come here again."

When Lalaji was released from the storeroom, he trembled like a watery 'kheer.' Munni Bai did not utter a word. He had been shamed into submission and monetary generosity towards his wife. She continued with the daily chores and spread the word that she needed a young, healthy maid, preferably with even features. From the very next day, likely candidates formed lines along the stair-way to the Lala's apartment.

Gulabo's vomiting stopped. A variety of powders from the Ayurvedic shop had no effect. "Shall we call the midwife," Durgi asked Hira. "She will do it quietly with a knitting needle. No one need know."

"She might kill Gulabo. We cannot let that happen. The neighbours will also talk. Find her a man. That is the safest." Hira had not forgotten the hundred rupees.

- -

Pale and weak, Gulabo sat under the roadside neem tree, taking in the fresh, cool, March air. She had been too nauseated to eat and the child within her did not show.

"Is that you Gulabo? Where have you been all this time? Where did you hide yourself?"

Sonu stood before her, his garbage cart parked by the side of the road. Gulabo looked down through thick lashes. "I have been very ill, as you can see."

"Where is Ramu? Do you have any children?"

"Ramu married Khamo. She has a beautiful son. They all live with Maamu at the village." She looked up at the young man and said shyly, "I have waited so long for you!"

Sonu's heart gave a leap. This was the girl of his dreams. Earlier she had been diffident to the point of rudeness. How wrong he had been! The love of his life had not married as she waited for him. It was all like a good Hindi film. He started humming "Dil wil, pyar wyar, mein kya janu re?"

My heart, my love, what do I know about all this? He put his arm around Gulabo and sat quietly, hoping that the bubble would not burst. It did, when the beat constable arrived and told the couple to get a shift on, unless they wanted to pay him a tenner to pretend he had not seen or heard anything.

Gulabo's spirits soared. She sat on Sonu's cycle cart, on a heap of salvaged plastic bags and waved a bright red rag in the air. She made sure they made love in the Mehta's cowshed on top of a stack of sweet smelling grass. Her unborn child had to have a father. She must have done something good in her life for God to have made things turn out so right.

Durgi and Hira celebrated the wedding with pomp and show, and lightning speed. The couple made a handsome pair. Gulabo looked delicate and beautiful in a rani pink salwar kameez. She wrapped a thick gold chain around Sonu's sinewy neck. Durgi and Hira doled out enough dowry for the bridegroom's new home. He seemed to have no close relatives, only friends. Lala Bharat Kumar's unborn progeny had found a legitimate home.

- -

Ravi finally badgered his parents into attending the PTA. Hira and Durgi did not sit in the class room although Shaku indicated that they should do so. They did not speak, nor were their eyes downcast. "We are almost as good as them," Durgi had muttered as husband and wife put on their best clothes.

"It is good to see you after so many years," Shaku told Durgi. "You both look well."

"It is because of your father young Memsahib. He saved my life" said Hira.

If she was surprised at this bit of information, Shaku did not show it. Over the past few years she had learnt to control her temper and calm down. Hakim had taught her milder, more sophisticated ways.

"Will you please sit down? It is so much easier to talk when you are seated." She called out to Manjit, the school ayah and asked for two glasses of tea. "Ravi is a bright boy. He will do well if he studies. I give him extra classes during break, but you have to make him complete his daily homework. Otherwise he will forget all that he learned in class."

Durgi was silent but Hira spoke. "We are illiterate. We cannot even write our names in Hindi let alone English. How can we teach him?"

Shaku could have kicked herself for having forgotten an obvious fact. She promised that Ravi would be helped to finish his work at school, and she would see to it. For the first time in her life, Durgi stood up as an equal and hugged young Memsahib. "Shukriya! Thank you for all that you have done!"

Shaku hugged her back saying, "Ravi will be an asset to you. I will see to that. You have nothing to worry about," and she saw them out through the spiked iron gate.

"Did you like Madamji?" Ravi asked.

"She is wonderful!" his mother replied. "She wants you to work hard to become a big 'affser.' Will you work more from today?" Ravi nodded. In the days after the PTA, his grades improved and by year end he stood first in the class. Twentyfive years later, he would be the first person from a servant line in Jullundur, to head a public sector company. But no one would ever let him forget his lowly origins. Success breeds jealousy and an empty belly spurs us on to greater heights, provided we can pull our-selves out of the mire first. That first step is the hardest and needs a lot of outside help. Ravi would always remain on the other side of the elite fence.

Later in years to follow, OBCs would spring up. Other Backward Classes would demand the same monetary and educational concessions awarded to the Harjans, also called the Dalits. These OBCs would flaunt their lower castes for the benefits offered, and in a country heaving and exhausted by trying to look after an uncontrollable population, higher castes would often try to change their designated class to avail quotas reserved for the lower classes. This would lead to a small scale industry in fake birth certificates, affidavits, school and college degrees, created and bought at exorbitant prices. Jobs would become scarce and admission into colleges, would be based only on almost perfect cent-per-cent results. The sub-castes would also become vociferous with their demands and a bureaucrat with the right ideas but minimal language skills, would differentiate between them as 'the creamy and the non-creamy layers.' This offensive and ambiguous term would creep into forms and registers stuffed away safely in government offices and record rooms, all a foundation for snail-paced work, insurmountable red tape and bribery.

- -

CHAPTER IX

"The manner of giving shows the character of the giver, more than the gift itself."... Lavater.

I COME BEARING GIFTS

"Isn't it time we made a baby too? Gulabo is pregnant; Khamo has a son; many of my college friends are onto seconds!" Shaku swung a slender leg across Hakim's thigh, as they lay in bed on a lazy Sunday morning. The winter sun streamed in through the window and tiny particles of dust, wool, and pollen could be seen floating down on the light slide.

Hakim touched her full lips with his fingers. That she was beside him, never ceased to amaze him. Years of silence, humiliation, servitude and a suspicious public attitude towards his faith, had made him reticent. But Shaku removed the silent walls, and opened him up to a life that was full and satisfying. She was a part of everything he did, the confident, gleaming pillar he could lean on. But the world was changing for the worse. Rabble rousers raved and ranted against the minorities. No one wanted to surrender an inch of space to those they considered outsiders. People, who had lived and worked on the sub-continent for centuries, were now made to feel that they did not have a place in the Indian nation. Strange reasons were touted. Christians were accused of converting Hindus for their own evil designs or as slaves of the expansionist ambitions attributed to the USA. All Muslims were believed to be against India and therefore her enemies. For the most trivial reasons, nuns were raped, priests killed and Muslims lynched. The real catalyst was general poverty and a lack of jobs. Christians were blamed for producing too many children with the sole purpose of taking over the Hindu state. Muslims were accused of the same thing but for a different Cause. They were creating a terrorist army, as were the Sikhs. The strident call was that Hinduism had to be protected for its bastions were falling. "Hindutva" was the new word coined to explain an ancient culture in its new avatar. A once tolerant people were held to ransom for the gains of a few. Safe ghettoes were springing up in corners of large cities to hold minority groups within high walls crowned with jagged shards of glass, locked in by spiked gates. Well trained, armed security guards protected them. No one asked why Lal Dhobi, the washer-man, named after his striped red and white shirt, produced seven children, or Mangra, the labourer did not practice family planning. The truth was that they relied on a large family to help with their trade and to increase their earnings. Another coal stoked iron plied by another member of the family meant another income added to a very lean kitty.

"Basically it is the fear of losing out," reasoned Hakim. "With the population increasing, and fewer jobs, it is hard to provide for a family dependant on a single salary. The overriding fear is that stomachs will not be filled. So to have more, we have to remove people who are considered extras, the imaginary purloiners of food and money. Sanjay Gandhi had the right notion about population control, but died before he could make a difference. The others are too gutless to pass strict laws like the Chinese. I wonder if this is the kind of insecure world I would like for my child."

Shaku looked deep into his eyes. "The whole world is becoming more dangerous, but that does not mean that children are not being produced. Our childhood was equally scary. Your grandfather went through hell. Look at us... we made it and happily too. Our child will be a living metaphor to our love."

"May Allah be praised!" said Hakim, ever grateful for a very pragmatic wife. He still prayed five times a day, but allowed Shaku to follow her own gods, rites and rituals. Her parents had taught him that a man's worth was his conscience, not his religion. Both families avoided dialogue on any faith and participated in each others festivities. This made life quite busy as India is a land of many festivals. Double these and the year seemed like a constant celebration, bolstered by specific festival foods. Shaku learned to prepare a good mutton biryani and Amina Bi made the best dal-ka-halwa. There were many priests and mullahs who found the Hindu-Muslim union repugnant. If the two families were aware of this, they did not react and pushed the thought away into some deep recesses of the mind.

Hakim was still not sure about creating a baby. His parents were eager to raise a grandchild. Deepak and Pushpa were concerned too and often asked Shaku if she had any gynae problems. She would laugh away their fears. However, she persisted with her demand and three months later, proudly told the family, "I think Hakim and I are going to have a baby!"

Two sets of would-be-grandparents, feverishly planned for the future child. Pushpa and Amina Bi knitted vests, booties and caps and hand-stitched tiny muslin garments for the hot weather. Deepak insisted on monthly check-ups and prescribed tonics, clubbed with a suitable diet. Mustapha was worried about the name... should it be Muslim or Hindu? Hakim bought a huge black and white, made-in-China panda. "It will smother the child!" laughed Shaku.

"Why do you worry so much Abba?" Hakim asked Mustapha. "There are so many names without any religious connotations. Make a list of those and all will be well." However, he could not convince the old man that in an increasingly intolerant society, the name was of no consequence.

True to her very positive, active lifestyle, Shaku did not allow the pregnancy to hamper her. She refused to lie down and rest. She still climbed the guava tree on hot summer days and ate tangerines straight off the trees. She sat on her haunches and made rotis and went to the Basti School daily. She did not suffer a day's nausea and her face glowed in anticipation of an event she had waited so long for. Pregnancy suited her and made her radiant.

It was with great difficulty that Deepak persuaded Shaku to stay at home the day she felt a twinge in the stomach. He drove her to the Bahadur Nursing Home and put her in the capable and trusted hands of his good friend Dr. Shakti Gurung. Deepak paced the hospital lobby as the contractions became more frequent. Though Shakti invited him for the birthing, he did not trust himself to participate in the delivery, being extremely nervous about seeing his only child going through pain. The two mothers and Mustapha stayed at home, preparing sweets in anticipation of the new arrival. Hakim sat on a hospital chair, reading a book on Gobar Gas Plants, as an alternative to fossil fuels. When Dr. Gurung walked in with a broad smile, both men caught his hands. "Is she all right?" asked Hakim.

"Was there a lot of pain?" Deepak inquired.

"Yes and no. Congratulations! You have achieved a double whammy!" the doctor said, grinning from ear to ear. "Come and meet your son and daughter." At a time when sonographs were non-existent, a glimpse into the mother's womb was impossible. The parents' only concern was safety. Most prayed for sons as they were the bearers of the family name. India would one day produce a breed of working women who would keep their maiden names in-spite of marriage. It was a moment in the distant future and would sometimes bring with it, traumatic repercussions.

Shaku was glowing. She lay propped up against several pillows and held the babies on either arm. "I have already named them. She is Luv and he is Khush. Neither name will reflect any religion. Tauji will be happy. Do you agree Hakim?"

The proud father did not say a word as he looked adoringly at her face. "Thank you my beloved wife, thank you for everything!"

When Shaku and the twins came home there were celebrations at the Bari Kothi. Friends came over, as did Durgi and her family. Neither the Baksh nor Batra clans sent congratulatory messages or gifts as they did not recognize Hakim and Shaku's union in the first place. How could they accept the existence of their children?

Shaku wanted to get back to the Basti as soon as possible. Feeding the twins was a long drawn out, continous chore. She asked Pushpa's opinion on getting a wet nurse. Deepak was in total agreement, but Amina Bi and Mustapha had their reservations. When Gulabo came to work, carrying her six month old son Chintu, they did not say anything but were upset. "How can Shaku allow her children to be suckled by that dreadful woman?" Amina Bi asked her son.

"They harmed you," added Mustapha to his son, reminiscing about incidents that took place not so very long ago.

In a rare display of affection, Hakim put his arms around his parents' shoulders and reassured them, "Abba and Ammi, please do not worry yourselves. Shaku is doing the right thing. Gulabo has learnt her lesson, and we cannot keep Shaku tied to the house. She has too much energy and will wilt if we keep her from her school. Let her go. Gulabo can handle the three infants."

"The children may pick up her awful habits!" Amina Bi declared.

"I have spoken to Sasoorji... he says nothing like that can happen through the milk."

His parents shook their heads in dismay but kept their counsel. They could not argue with people who had nurtured them over three generations. They had to trust their judgment, for they were far from a land called 'home.'

Gulabo, healthy and strong, beloved wife of the garbage collector Sonu, nursed the Baksh twins as her own. Durgi helped her with the nappies and baths. Hira moved back with his precious rickshaw. Ruby was married off to Ramu's younger brother. Ravi was doing well at the Basti School. He was likely to win a scholarship for excellence, created in memory of Vaid Hari Baksh, the visionary, who through his kindness had sown the seeds of a new order.

- -

Shaku was driven to the school by her father. Gulabo and the three babies went too. There were garlands of sacred marigolds strung on the gate. Colourful balloons hung from the doorways and popped each time there was a gust of wind and they scraped the rough walls. The babies had to be shown in every classroom where the children touched them and the teachers made it a point to hold them. The miracle of identical twins created a feeling of awe and wonder.

Gulabo and her son Chintu, went un-noticed as she sat feeding him in an empty class-room.

Deepak brought out a dozen boxes of sweets and distributed them amongst everyone on the premises. The school felt honoured and special on being introduced to the twins. After tea, the senior most health promoter brought a gift, neatly packed in red and blue cellophane. "You should not have done this!" said Shaku, knowing that money for this must have been collected from each one's meager resources.

"Why not?" asked Vinod. "Aren't they our children too?"

"Of course they are, but you have spent so much on the decorations and now this gift."

"Open it Madamji," suggested Mohini, who had been assigned the task of buying the garments. Shaku opened the parcel and held up the blue and pink frocks with matching bonnets. Acceding to numerous requests, she and Gulabo dressed the babies in their new clothes.

There was a sudden clamour at the gate. Commando swaggered in holding Vijay's hand. "Sorry I am late, Madamji. I knew you were coming but someone came to see me... someone needing help." He held Luv, kissed her on the brow and placed a folded hundred rupee note in her tiny hand. She clenched it with all her might. Then he picked up Khush and did the same thing. Shaku protested. "You are giving them too much. Just a one rupee coin will do."

Commando's eyes flashed, "Madamji, your children are my children. No one can harm them as long as I live. At Luv's wedding, I shall shower thousands of rupees on her, not a paltry hundred!" In his own way he had told her of his worth.

Shaku knew she had hurt his pride by questioning the amount he had given. She meant to show consideration but he thought otherwise. She made up for the mistake by putting a laddu in his mouth. "You shall be her Maamu and my brother at the wedding," she promised. She knew that by holding the twins and blessing them with cash, Commando had conveyed to the slum that the children and she were under his protection. There was a deep symbolism in his actions. The Basti understood this, she had not. The understanding of this made her feel very warm and secure.

"You should have seen the reception they got!" said Shaku enthusiastically, describing the visit to Hakim.

"I hope they do not pick up an infection. The slum is a very dirty place."

"Baba will deal with that, if it happens. They are so loving and humble there. Everyone seems to belong to one big family. I would like the twins to be so too. Even when they go to school, I shall keep taking them there so that they realize how the other side lives."

Hakim looked into the distance. "I would like to take them home for a visit."

"Home?" asked Shaku, failing to understand what he said.

"To the land of my forefathers. Just a visit, nothing more."

"We must go the moment they can take the journey," smiled Shaku. "I too would love to see Kandahar. Tauji describes it so well!"

The idea grew but lay buried in their minds. When the twins were three years old, Hakim and Shaku decided to go to Kandahar. Mustapha insisted on accompanying them. Deepak felt the twins would not be able to bear the rigors of Afghanistan.

"There is plenty of time for further visits. Leave them here. You three ought to make the visit, see the place and prepare yourselves for the next trip with them. Amina Bi and Pushpa will manage them here. And of course, Gulabo is like a second mother to them."

Shaku felt a strange fluttering in her stomach. She pushed it aside. Her father's remarks had roused an unwanted feeling within her. She did not want to share her babies with Gulabo. Honest as ever, she told Hakim of her feelings, reasoning at the same time that she was being unfair.

"I love the way you turn every idea on its head and look at all sides! It's natural that you feel upset. You are going to miss them. You can stay back if you want, but Abba and I must go. I promised him this trip long ago and want him to see his home again before he passes on."

"I shall go too. Forget that I said anything about anything! It was just a passing twinge of jealousy"

Shaku, Hakim and Mustapha left for Afghanistan in April. The journey was long and tedious. After travelling to the farthest railhead the Indian Railways offered, the travelers took rickety buses, rattling taxis, tongas, half starved donkeys and any other mode of transport they could hitch a ride on. It was advisable that Shaku wore a sky blue, flowing burkha, as was the way of Afghan women. Initially, it took a little getting used to, but soon she started enjoying the safety of the cocoon surrounding her. She saw the whole world through a net window, but no one could observe her. Used to men staring long and hard at her face, she found the anonymity of the burkha a pleasant reprieve.

The sharp wind was something Shaku had never experienced before. It blew throughout the day, carrying swathes of dust in its wake. Roads were practically non-existent, but the surrounding peaks more than made up these short comings with their rock covered, gigantic magnificence. The dry, dusty plains of Kandahar had stands of trees. On closer examination they turned out to be loaded with apricots, almonds and pomegranates. It was a stark moonscape, awesome in rather a forbidding way.

"I am glad we did not bring the twins," said Hakim. They sat by the roadside, sipping chai, waiting for a bus to take them into the distant hills. Hakim handed his father a fistful of apricots and smiled as the old man relished each one, saving the woody seeds to be cracked later on for the almonds. Back home in Jullundur they would have to pay exorbitant prices for apricot almonds of this flavour.

"This is my land!" Mustapha stated the fact with pride and satisfaction. "Thank you son!"

"I love it!" declared Shaku, ever ready to enjoy any challenge that came her way.

"Are you sure?" asked Hakim. "No running water, no proper toilets, no eating places. This is a far cry from your beloved Jullundur."

"It is no worse than the Basti. I can live with that," she pointed towards the surrounding areas. "The people are friendly and warm. They speak with sincerity, just as at the Basti. Progress often takes away from people rather than add to their values. It makes them selfish and self-centred not generous and kind."

Mustapha smiled. "I am glad you like them. They do not seem to have changed much since my childhood."

A huge cloud of dust heralded their bus. Sitting amongst baskets of apricots, vegetables, potatoes, live chickens, eggs, grapes and smelly passengers, Shaku felt as if she was living in a dream, far from the reality of Jullundur, the Basti and the twins. The last phone call, made over a patchy, crackling line at the local post office, had assured her that all was well at the Bari Kothi. The bus headed towards the village Khas, nestled amongst a patch of green trees and brilliant yellow mustard fields, at the foot of the huge mountains. The houses were mud coloured and hardly distinguishable from the surrounding areas. It was this village from where Mustapha had set out with his father, the money-lender, almost five decades earlier He had finally come home but had not been able to fulfill his promise to Amina Bi. He would make up to her on the next visit.

The bus took much longer than anticipated to reach the village that appeared so near from the chai shop. The road was 'kutcha' and had been washed away in the last heavy rain, which was practically history in these parts. It was covered with loose boulders and the driver's sole aim was not to let the tyres rip, so they moved at a snail's pace. Shaku shuddered to think of the onward journey the rest of the passengers would face. A small group of three men, and two women in deep blue burkhas, waited at the bus stop.

After much bargaining, they bought a couple of chickens and some vegetables off the passengers.

It was only after the bus left that the three travelers realized the group had come to receive them. The men exchanged bear hugs and shook hands. The women were gentler but as excited to meet their relative-by-marriage. Jalal, Tariq and Ahmed were Mustapha's cousins, his father's nephews. Their grizzled hair and parched skin made them look older than they were. Jehan was Tariq's wife and Aziza their daughter. Both chattered like the noisy babblers or "seven sisters" Shaku had left in the fruit trees at home. As they walked towards the village, chickens squawking, vegetables and baggage held in their arms, the group exchanged the news of many years. The money-lender had never returned home. Mustapha was silent, seeking closure but finding none. No one could give him any news of his father.

The whole village came to greet them. After the evening meal, the women went into a small carpeted room and took off their burkhas. They hung them on wooden pegs and looked at each other in the light of a hurricane lamp that hung from the ceiling. Unlike their men, they had smooth, well-tended skins. Aziza, almost as old as Shaku, had Grecian features, inherited from the blood line injected by one of Alexander's troops.

"You are beautiful!" she said, sliding slender fingers down Shaku's cheeks.

"So are you." They talked late into the night, exchanging details of a land far away, children left behind and a different way of life. Shaku showed them photographs of the school and the twins.

"I wish I could have studied," sighed Aziza.

"Didn't you?" Shaku was surprised.

"There is no school here and Kabul is too far. Abba taught me a little Farsi but I do not even know the English alphabet!" she declared with disgust.

"I shall start teaching you in the morning," said Shaku.

"Go to sleep now," said Jehan, drawing up the quilts. "There is plenty of time."

But there was very little time. The two week visit flew on the wheels of constant activity and hours of catching up on news. There was so much to do, so much to say, families to visit and celebratory feasts to be prepared. Aziza and Shaku would sit with paper and pencil early in the morning, before anyone stirred and then again, late at night, under the hurricane lamp. Towards the end, Shaku filled empty pages with alphabets to be copied, two and three letter words to be inscribed, all re-written in Farsi so that her pupil could recognize the sounds and meanings. She advised Aziza to listen to the BBC news on the radio and copy the accents of the anchors. She promised to return the following year to check and continue with the lessons.

It saddened both families to see each other go. As they under-took the arduous journey once again, each was silent, deep in their own thoughts. Mustapha wondered if he would ever be able to bring Amina Bi as promised. He had relished every moment of the visit. He belonged to this village, to Afghanistan, to the fields and the fruit trees. This was home, but destiny had left him in another land which refused to accept him even though he had given his life to its well being.

Shaku started planning for her next visit. She was appalled at the primitive conditions, the lack of schools and basic amenities. These people who were so brave, cheerful, hospitable, hard-working, deserved better. If she could contribute a little to her new found family, it would make her life more worthwhile. She would and could go beyond the Basti by dividing time between the two countries.

Often life throws up some invisible saints, catalysts for change, extraordinary individuals who think beyond themselves, to lead the world towards better ways and thoughts. Shaku was one such individual. Her inheritance came from a grandfather who looked beyond his caste and extended a helping hand to a stranger; from a grandmother who had phenomenal strength in bearing the burdens of an often difficult, ritual dictated world; from a father who continued a tolerant tradition, stood up for the truth and added intellectual prowess; from a mother who was kind, affectionate and realistic about the changing family scene. Shaku had no doubt that these qualities went way back in time, well beyond and before the tiny circle of individuals she loved. Such people do not make the headlines or appear on screens, but they are the backbone of a nation, the unknown heroes of their times.

She rummaged in her bag for a vial of Vaseline. She smeared it on her dry lips thinking of Aziza, who had to use fresh butter instead. The village of Khas was so far removed from the existing world, caught up in a charming but uncomfortable time warp. It was her challenge to bring a few changes, however small. She had made a good beginning with Aziza.

As Shaku elaborated her plans for the future, Hakim smiled. "Don't plan so far ahead. We shall see about things next year. The twins are still too young for this kind of journey or place."

Shaku put her head on his shoulder, secure in the knowledge that he would always be by her side in whatever she undertook. She dozed off in-spite of a bus that shook like a bag of marbles.

- -

CHAPTER X

"There is always room for a man of force, and he makes room for many."... Emerson.

COMMANDO'S TALE

Commando's presence at the school became more frequent. He attended the PTA meetings in place of Vijay's parents, and the little boy looked more and more like him. The same swagger, dress style, slow deliberate talk, were adopted by the little chela. This amused and pleased the guru.

"Vijay's calmed down," observed Shaku with satisfaction.

"What do you attribute it to?" asked Hakim.

"Commando's company. He is a sobering influence. He stays in the same house and the nephew worships him. The tantrums and destruction has stopped; he is reading and writing better."

"I caught a glimpse of this man in the market, the day you pointed him out at the jeweler's shop. Looks a thug to me; nothing soft or kind about him. I'd be careful if I were you."

Be careful of what?" Shaku laughed as she put the question to him. "You aren't jealous of him are you?"

"A typical woman's remark, one not worth bothering about! It's just that I have seen his kind in the streets and they command through cruelty and brutal persuasion, not love. Haven't you ever wondered how he got that sobriquet?"

"He is a leader. Come to the Basti and see for yourself. The colony worships him."

"Worships or fears?" questioned her husband.

- -

Commando grew up on the streets of Mai Phoolan Gate. The youngest amongst seven children... four girls and three boys, he was puny and sickly. No one expected him to live, but he had tremendous survival instincts. If Devki forgot to feed him, he would bawl continuously for attention. "Feed that child or throw him in the well!" his father Bhujbal roared. "I must have my sleep." The man manufactured moonshine, a task performed at night, in the dark shadows of a broken down asbestos shed. Just to keep the child quiet, one or the other of the lactating mothers' at the 'havelli,' quietened him with a suckle. The power of the child's lungs, probably inherited from his father, earned him the name "Commando." He grew strong and tall with the immunity of many women and the richness of their milk. He refused to be cowed down by his father.

Bhujbal's liquor sold well and was exported to other states too. When Prohibition was introduced, the women of the havelli set up a flower shop. Prospective customers were handed sweet scented bouquets wrapped around bottles of 'tharra' and 'santra,' so named because of its deep orange colour and smell. Everyone in the havelli was involved in some task related to making liquor. Money flowed in, so no one complained. The occasional policeman, who chanced upon the shed, usually through the strong orange smell wafting on the evening breeze, left happy, well looked after and very drunk. By the age of three, Commando had the first sip of his father's produce. Bhujbal laughed uproariously as the child, talking gibberish, staggered across the bedroom into Devki's arms. Too frightened to say anything, the mother started talking to her youngest, describing the horrors of too much liquor. Commando listened carefully but learnt to keep both parents happy. He never drank much as he realized that Bhujbal's weakness was a loss of control over mind and senses after a good binge. That was the moment when others took advantage of the strong man. The women and children stole small amounts of cash, and the servants pinched packets of liquor and slept soundly.

The bricked in streets of Mai Phoolan Gate, were Commando's playing field. He learned cricket, football and 'kanchas' or marbles in the narrow lanes that allowed people to walk two abreast and no more. He rode his first cycle in the same lanes and was adept at disappearing into side streets if he saw policemen or the neighbourhood bullies. By the age of ten he was gambling at marbles and won most times. Bhujbal was quick to recognize his youngest son's intelligence, quick wit and strength. He made him his natural heir and by the time he lay dying of Heart Disease and Diabetes, Commando knew everything there was to know of the business.

"You fish faced 'dhobin,' who do you think you are? How dare you say my son made eyes at your daughter? She looks even worse than you!"

Commando looked up and saw that his youngest 'bua' was hurling invective at the neighbour across the street. The fight was going on through the third storey windows of the houses that faced each other.

"Come down you fat cow and I shall twist your tail," shouted the neighbour. "I shall gouge out your son's moony eyes, even if he lifts them up to look at my girl!"

Commando's aunt was virtually frothing at the mouth. From various levels of the building, women and children looked upwards, out of their windows and laughed at the 'tamaasha.' A free show like this enlivened the tedium of the day in homes where there was nothing to do once the household chores were over.

The aunt disappeared from the window and returned with a basket of melon peels and kitchen garbage. She took aim and flung the missile. Her surprised foe fell backwards, blinded by the goo. Commando laughed aloud but swore he would be out of Mai Phoolan Gate the day he could build a house in a newer part of town. He climbed the narrow stairs of the havelli to the third floor and locked his aunt in the bath room.

The vanquished neighbour washed herself and reappeared at her window, shouting hysterically. "So you threw melon seeds on me to show that you bought the most expensive fruit first? Come out you cow, and I shall hit your ugly mug with the priciest mango stones of the season!" But of course, the rival did not appear. After an hour or so, with no retaliation from the opposite side, her shrill cries petered down and she went to bed to rest with a cold compress on her brow. Commando unlocked his aunt, did not say a word but had made his point.

Bhujbal left no will or letter to say who should take over the liquor business. However, he did call the family around his death-bed and told them he was entrusting Commando to be the head of the family. A man of strong principles, Commando did just that. He took charge and distributed his father's fortune equally amongst his siblings. "Make more out of this," he commanded as he handed out red velvet bags of lucre and gold jewelry. His eldest brother, Vijay's father, was the first to transit out of the area. He bought a small plot of land at Naya Gaon... or the 'New Village,' and built a straw-roofed shack with his own hands. The rest of the family continued to stay at the ancestral home, launching their children into the world from there. Commando took his chance and moved in with his brother as he supervised the making of a palatial house on a huge piece of land nearby. He built another complete unit on the top floor and handed the keys to his bhabi... who he sympathized with... saying, "This is for looking after me." Though he knew that his brother had strayed and produced a daughter out of wedlock, he never talked about the incident. The ground floor he kept for himself and welcomed any member of his extended family whenever they decided to visit. With six large bedrooms and 'bhaiya's' apartment on the top floor, there was never a shortage of space. He fixed a huge red granite plaque at the gate with screwed in brass letters that read, "Commando's Palace."

An early teenage relationship behind him, Commando took his time looking for a girl. He wanted a convent educated one to look after his new bungalow and bring sophisticated ways into his life. Not having gone beyond the fifth class at the Mai Phoolan Devi Public School, he felt a wife's educational degrees would open doors with the bureaucracy and in elite circles. As Bhujbal had passed on, Devki took it upon herself to find a suitable bride for her youngest son. She could not understand Commando's polite rejection of every prospective, whose photograph she placed before him. Commando scanned marital advertisements in the Sunday papers.

"Beautiful, fair, slim, convent educated girl, 19 years old; well-versed in household affairs; respectable parents;

father in government service; brother in USA; early marriage required; modest dowry offered."

Commando carefully cut out the notification, noted the box number and landed at Renuka Didee's house one morning. He liked the girl who served him tea. "We cannot give much dowry," said Ravinder Didee apologetically. "Educating Satinder in the USA is very expensive."

"Uncleji, have I asked for any?" asked Commando. "I have so much that I need no dowry-showry from anyone, just a wife!" Renuka smiled at him. She liked his swarthy looks and obvious charisma. He appeared rich too. What more could a girl ask for?

"What do you do son?" asked Meera, the mother.

"Auntyji, I own some businesses dealing with property and beverages."

"A realtor? And do you own the beverage factory?"

"Of course I own these businesses otherwise why would I look for a convent educated girl?"

"Why are you called Commando?"

"My name is Kamandev Singh, but my father thought Commando was more impressive."

"Which name should we use on the card?" asked Ravinder, a stickler for details.

"Uncleji, you leave it to me. I shall print the cards."

As Renuka had been rejected several times by parents who discussed the terms of dowry first and marriage later, the unexpected arrival of Commando was a relief.

When Satinder Didee flew in from the USA, he was suspicious. "Why do you allow him to pay for everything? Have a small wedding according to our means, but let us foot the bill."

His father brushed away all opposition. "We can hardly afford your education! The man is good and rich. These small amounts do not matter to him."

"We shall never be able to hold our heads up if this gets out!"

"Son, when you get a job and start earning, we will hold our heads higher than anyone else."

Though the Didee's did not like Commando's address, they knew the area would be developed within a few years. Property and gold were the two most precious commodities. With an ever increasing populace, real estate would never suffice and land prices would soar. Their daughter would be comfortable. Love would enter the scene later on. They made some discreet enquiries at Naya Gaon. Everyone was full of praise for Commando. He was generous, kind, powerful. He looked after his family, boasted a bit but seemed to have very paying 'dhandas' or businesses. No one knew where exactly his factory was or what exactly he did. That he threw lavish parties was a known fact. Devki was a bit of a shock to Renuka, but her parents hardly paid any notice to her doubts. "Most mothers-in-law are unattractive," Meera assured her daughter. "Just humour her and all will be well. Never, never argue with her. She will eat you alive."

"He's not a 'badmash' or 'goonda,' is he?" Ravinder asked an elderly lady, who owned a large house next to Commando's Palace.

"Certainly not! Would a bad man have taken my husband to the hospital the day he had a heart attack? He fell in the bathroom and I could not lift him by myself. I ran out screaming for help. Commando came immediately. I can tell you so many wonderful stories about him…"

"Not now Behanji. You have helped a lot. We all shall have plenty of time after the wedding." Ravinder extricated himself with speed.

Satisfied that they had made the right choice, the Didees started planning the wedding. Commando was in and out of their home. He did not want anything at all from the in-laws. He took Renuka out to the best shops, bought her saris, jewelry, footwear and a huge vanity case, everything a rich bride would buy to show the neighbours, not neccessarily to use. As the great day drew near, Renuka fell more and more in love with her fiancee`. She loved his soft voice, loud laughter and swagger. He was the epitome of masculinity. His generosity knew no bounds. She would learn to tolerate the constant boasting.

- -

Commando placed an oversized, red, saffron scented envelope, inscribed in gold, on Shaku's desk. Under it was a box of almonds.

"So you are going in for a love marriage?" teased the Principal of the Basti School.

"Sort of," the young man looked shy and awkward. "You will come, won't you? And Bhaiya and the twins too?"

"I would not miss this wedding for anything. You ought to go to Kashmir for your honeymoon. Renuka will love it. I can arrange a houseboat for you. It's called the Taj Mahal. I shall fix it with the owner, Bashir Ahmed."

"You do that Madamji. You must have had a wonderful time there." It was his turn to tease her.

The wedding was a lavish affair. The neighbourhood talked about it for years. Commando, dressed in a gold brocade 'sherwani' sat astride a white mare. Clutching his uncle's waist and dressed in a similar fashion, was his 'sarbala,' little Vijay, who carried his beloved Chacha's dress sword. Commando sat gingerly on the horse for he had never ridden one before. But one day's glory astride a horse with the heroic photographs that followed, was enough compensation.

The bride was exquisite in a scarlet lehnga with gold 'kaleeras' on her wrists. A diamond 'nathni' hung from her nose and she wore at least a kilogram of ornaments around her neck, hands and ankles. This was as per Commando's instructions. "Money with a gun to back it, brings power," he said. "Let them all see we have the cash. The rest will follow."

After the ceremony, a photographer made the young couple strike romantic poses for photographs for the wedding album. Many pictures were focused on Shaku, Hakim and the twins.

Bashir Ahmed festooned the Taj Mahal with buntings and flowers. He knew of Commando through his network of shawl and carpet sellers, who descended on the plains of Punjab in winter. They went from door to door, selling their wares, looking for people who could help the Cause.

Bashir gestured to Commando. "Where is Mem Sahib?"

"Sleeping."

"Let her sleep. I know that honeymooners get very tired," he winked. "Come with me Sahib. I have something to show you."

They used Bashir's 'shikaara' to row across to a house on the far side of the lake. Over a cup of steaming 'kahva,'... spiced tea, Bashir's brother showed Commando a bucketful of the purest heroin. Percentages were fixed, drop locations pin pointed, hands shaken. Commando was into a new 'dhanda.' On his return to Jullundur, he closed down the distillery, bought five new flats in the best localities and reassigned jobs in an already established network. The switch was easy.

Having learnt his lessons from the extended family at Mai Phoolan Gate, Commando proved to be a good husband. He looked after Renuka and catered to all her needs. He never beat her but demanded unquestioning obedience. He did not discuss his work scene with her or anyone else. Their safety lay in not knowing. He allowed her to meet her friends, go to the market, movies and kitty parties. He knew she was safe because his people were in every part of Naya Gaon and the city. They would watch over her. When he was at home he expected her to be there too. The same safety net extended over his family and friends. He would disappear over long stretches of time and never reveal where he had been. Under Commando's strict and strangely benign eye, the Basti seldom saw much criminal activity, the like of which was found in the town, policed by the state.

Within the year Commando started carrying and delivering IED's (improvised explosive devices). He did not ask his contacts where they would be used. He did not pass judgment on the rightness or wrongness of an action. When civilians were killed in a crowded market at Delhi or a train in Bombay, it was as tragic an event as young men shot in Kashmir by the security forces because they were suspected militants. In Commando's eyes, all deliberate killing left grief-stricken families and unanswered questions, but they were necessary. The same coin reflected both sides. Your sorrow was determined by which side of the coin you viewed. The militant did what he did because he felt it was right. The security forces did their duty to keep the nation safe. In both cases, power lay at the end of a barrel which was the biggest tool for barter and financial gain. He often wondered why problems could not be worked out through the oldest ploys in the world, dialogue, persuasion and education. He also knew that such stratagems would take away his substantial income. But for his numerous dhandas, he and his family would be on the roads, sleeping on foot paths, under bridges, and defecating in open spaces. Was it wrong if he earned money by any means he could? If the state could not provide him basic amenities then he would grab whatever he could and in whichever manner. Well-being and family alone dictated his modus operandi.

Renuka brought class and sophistication to Commando's Palace. She scoured the markets for objects de art and the best artists were displayed on her walls. She could serve a six course sit-down meal or lay out a barbeque and buffet along with 'sarson-tha-saag' and 'makki-di-roti.' She was the perfect mate for a man in a hurry, who wanted the doors of power to open into an ever widening business arena. "What does your husband do?" an English woman asked as she drank wine from a fluted glass.

"He is a realtor. He is also into pharmaceuticals. I am afraid I don't know much about his business... but he is a good husband," she assured her guest, "for he does not beat me!" The English woman was shocked that beatings were still a topic for discussion and that Indian women still did not hit back.

The day Bindiya was born, Commando unwrapped a thick gold chain with a large emerald pendant, from a piece of red tissue paper. As he clasped it round Renuka's neck he whispered, "Thank you for being the perfect wife. Now we have to make our daughter just like you."

"And if we have a son? I will make him just like you." She answered her own question and knew he was pleased.

- -

CHAPTER XI

"Responsibilities gravitate to the person who can shoulder them; power flows to the man who knows how."... Elbert Hubbard.

ST. PHILLIPS

Shaku tutored Durgi's son for over a year. Ravi studied hard, came first in his class and spoke the Queen's English. After all he did listen to the news on BBC as suggested by Madamji. He sat for the admission test at St. Phillip's Academy and passed with flying colours. The Principal, Peter Gomes shook his hand and welcomed him aboard. He was introduced to his peers in Class III as "Ravi Hira."

The room was crammed with over fifty children, thirty-five boys and twenty two girls. Principal Gomes approved of co-education, even though it was a new concept. He believed children grew up more balanced if they mingled with the opposite sex. In deference to parents' wishes, girls sat on one side of the room and boys on the other. Few words were exchanged between the groups. Gomes felt he had to break gender barriers for a more equal future. When inter-gender, inter-class soccer was introduced, the boys played rough and the girls cried. Within a couple of weeks, the girls ganged up and kicked the boys around. Except for band-aid and kind words, both teams were given no quarter whatsoever.

Another member of the team was Vijay, Commando's nephew. A class junior to Ravi, he joined the team as much for his confidence as for spirited play. He was afraid of nothing, no one and not very keen on academics. The two boys used the same auto-rickshaw and became friends. Vijay did the talking, while Ravi listened. They shared their tiffins during lunch break.

"Why is India called a peninsula?" asked the Geography teacher on the first day of school. Very few hands were raised. One of them was Ravi's. "Tell me son," the teacher encouraged the boy. When he answered correctly she told the class to clap in appreciation. "He has come from Naya Gaon. You know what that means? You all have better homes but do no work. You ought to be ashamed of yourselves." The very patronizing, thoughtless introduction to the new entrant, made him a target for ridicule and ragging. His Naya Gaon address revealed his lower strata in society. During break he sat alone and tried to swallow the paratha and 'alu' made by Durgi. It stuck in his throat and tasted like a lump of gloy. A small group of boys passed by. They did not look at him but flung a fistful of sand into his lunch box. Ravi packed his tiffin and took it home.

"Who did this?" asked Durgi as she threw away the wasted food.

"Some boys."

"Give me their names and I shall sort out their parents!"

"You must not do anything of the sort," Hira advised. "We do not want fights. Give him time and he will settle down. If you interfere they will target him more."

Durgi hugged her son and rumpled his hair. "You will settle down, but will they?"

The second day was no better than the first. The moment the teacher's back was turned, bits of chalk flew at Ravi. Beant, his desk partner, sqeezed himself next to two other boys. The teacher was furious. "Get back to your seat. Why have you exchanged desks?"

"Miss, he farts!" said Beant. The girls giggled into their handkerchiefs. The teacher brought in another desk and Ravi sat alone, without a partner.

"I did not fart Ma. But they humiliated me. What have we done that they treat us so?"

"Nothing my son," responded Hira. "This is centuries of ingrained stupidity. You are as good as them, if not better, but we all pay the price for our ancestor's caste."

"I shall go to the school tomorrow," fumed Durgi, ever ready to take up the family cause. "I shall rub Beant's nose in the dirt and spit on his mother's face! Our money is the same colour as theirs. How dare they?"

Ravi was frightened. "Don't let her go Bapu!" he pleaded. "They will ask me to leave the school and I will never become a big officer."

Hira assured him that his mother would do no such thing.

Ravi's first few weeks were unbearable. He stopped eating or doing his homework. Grades fell and he cried into the pillow at night. That is till Vijay joined him at tiffin time.

"Don't worry! My Chacha has taught me how to deal with these haramzaadas.' During games we shall corner him, drop him on the soccer field, then kick him in the stomach. Make it all look like proper play."

The referee blew long on the whistle and asked for a break. An injured player lay on the ground, clutching his stomach, writhing in pain. He screamed and went on pointing towards two backs in the distance. Ravi and Vijay laughed as they peed in the toilet. Beant did not attend school for a week. In class he promised retribution in Ravi's ear.

As a result of that particular soccer match, the girls started vying for the Naya Gaon boys' attention. There is something very primeval in our reactive instincts. The vanquisher is all powerful. We flock to him as we feel secure in his shadow and by his side. The vanquished leads a lonely, friendless life. Vijay taught Ravi that conquests can only be made through brute strength backed by strategic cunning. This is the first rule of survival at the slum.

Ravi began smiling again. His grades improved. Vijay and he were inseparable.

The Hindi teacher was not happy with Ravi. She lived at Naya Gaon, in a home a fraction of the size of Commando's Palace. When she came to know that Ravi and Vijay were always seen together, she started picking on both of them.

"Come here Ravi. Is this how you spell 'aavashya?' Write the word out fifty times during the break." She put a huge red cross across the page rather than on the one incorrect word. When Vijay came looking for his friend, she made him stand in the sun and refused to let him eat his tiffin. The boys were stoic about their punishment and did not report it at home.

A week later, Vijay failed to write the alphabet in order. A pencil was used to twist his ear, leaving red welts. A ruler swished onto his open palm. He did not flinch or even withdraw his hand. But he did put a tin tack on the teacher's chair, kept in place with a moistened bit of parantha. The act was done with the whole class watching. They laughed with delight as Mrs. Goel was an unpopular teacher. She came, nodded her acknowledgement of their greetings and sat down to teach. She rose again, screaming, a tin tack protruding out of her rather substantial butt. The Principal was brought in, and asked who had done such a dastardly deed. In unison, the class stood up and pointed at Vijay. The Principal suspended the little boy immediately.

When Commando arrived at the office and asked to see the Head, he was told to make an appointment as the Principal was out. He walked into Peter Gomes' office without knocking, and sat down opposite him without being given permission to do so. Very deliberately he put his feet on Gomes' polished desk. Gomes was beside himself with anger. He stood up, glaring at Commando. "Who are you and how have you barged into my room! Guards!" he sputtered. "Remove this man at once!"

Emmanuel, the sole guard appeared. He saw Commando and stood at attention, speechless. He lowered his eyes and did nothing. "Why are you just standing there? Remove this man! I shall call the police." His hands shook as he dialed 100. A muscular hand covered his and the mouth piece was returned to the cradle.

"I am Commando. You may not have heard of me."

Gomes sat down and gestured towards Emmanuel, asking him to leave the room.

Commando removed his feet off the desk. "About my nephew Vijay..." he drawled in a soft voice.

"Who are you? And what have you to do with Vijay? Where are his parents? I want to talk to them! How dare you enter my office without permission?"

"I just told you I am Commando." The tone was deliberate and menacing. "Forget his parents. I am his Chacha. I am here talking to you."

"We cannot tolerate indiscipline. Mrs. Goel has not come to work. She is most hurt!" blustered Gomes. "We have been kind enough to take in your children from the slums, but that does not mean they can bring the same atmosphere here."

"Oye, Principalji, don't talk to me about the slum. Come and see my house. This school would fit into it. And you have taken children from the slums because the Government has told you to do so. You need to adjust to the ways of kids from Naya Gaon, not us to you. Mrs. Goel ought to be dismissed for meting out corporal punishment. Tell her so. She knows who I am." Commando got up to go. He looked Gomes in the eye and said, "Next time don't call your lackeys. They maybe your employees but owe their allegiance to me. I will be sending Vijay to class tomorrow. He has missed enough!"

Mrs Goel heard about Commando's visit. Vijay was reinstalled and was not picked on by the teacher any more. She gave him surprisingly good marks in spite of bad work.

Ravi was not so fortunate. The teachers confabulated in the staff room. They had the tacit approval of the Principal in evolving plans to remove the Basti children from the school. Gomes considered them a threat and he used the parental angle to support his ideas. Mrs. Rathore, wife of an IAS (Indian Administrative Service) officer, sought an interview. She was accompanied by Mrs B. Singh and Mrs. Antia. All had children in Ravi's class. Mrs. Rathore fired the first salvo. "We do not want our children to sit with any junglee children from the Basti. Their language is foul, their manners uncouth, bodies unclean. We are paying your school good money for our children's education. Open another section for the weaker students." She was careful not to mention Ravi or Vijay or the words "Dalit" and "Harijan." Gomes had warned them that his walls had ears.

"My daughter came home with lice. My maid washes her hair daily. I examine her hair daily. How can my daughter's hair be infested? It is due to these children from Naya Gaon. You must do something or I shall withdraw my child from your school." Mrs. Singh threatened. Her use of the personal pronoun repeatedly showed how important she felt.

Mrs. Antia, a clever woman, adopted a different line, a sympathetic one. "We feel sorry for these children. We all realize they have to be absorbed in our society. We understand that. They hardly pay any fees as they are subsidized by the state. Either open another school for them in the vernacular, or increase their fees so that they quit the English medium school."

Gomes put the matter to the School Governing Board. That august body, whose members only delivered speeches, attended functions and handed out prizes for which they made it to Page 3 of the dailies, decided that a vernacular section would solve all problems.

Vijay and Ravi found themselves under a temporary shed with a tin roof, no fans, no walls and broken desks. They loved the open space, the clubbing together of Classes I and II and the easier curriculum. With twenty five other children, they felt more comfortable, forgot their manners and English and played with the two un-trained teachers who were employed at half rates.

"It is getting very hot in the class," Ravi mentioned to Durgi.

"Switch on the fans."

"We have none in the shed."

"Which shed?" his mother asked.

Bit by bit the whole sordid story poured out of the mouth of a child who till then was happiest playing with his own kind and saw nothing wrong in the arrangement.

Durgi was seething. "I shall go to Commando!" she declared.

Gomes tried to explain to the angry man, who thumped the table and stood over him, that all this had been done to accommodate the Basti children in a friendlier, more familiar atmosphere, not to discriminate against them.

"You mean you've done this so that they never learn better things or get the advantages richer people have? If, and I repeat if, the children are not back again by next week, and your sheds dismantled, you shall have Commando to deal with."

"He is a bully and a thorn in my side." Gomes whined to the Board. "You have to approach the police to deal with him."

The Board did one better and led a delegation to the State Education Minister. Commando had pre-empted their move and already paid his respects at that office with a small box of sweets over an underlay of gold coins. The minister listened patiently and said, "I may have to revoke the recognition given to the school for various malpractices brought to my notice. You seem to have forgotten the mandate that 25% of your children should be from the Economically Weaker Sections. That is imperative. However, if you like I can ask the police to investigate your complaint."

"But Sirji, we did put 25% EWS children under sheds. Gomes saw to that and is busy bringing up their English language, personally!" one of the members protested.

"I want to hear nothing more! Sort it out or else..."

The Board withdrew their petition, touched his feet and thanked him for his precious time and patient hearing. As they got into their cars, the spokesman said, "Gomes, do try to deal with these minor matters on your own. Do not bring them before the Board." They received too many perks from the school to be able to afford its closure. Gomes was distraught as he repeated a litany of woes before his wife Belinda Maria.

"Stop worrying Daaahling," she drawled. "If they can't help you, join the enemy. Commando will be far more useful to the school than a group of fat, greasy, disinterested businessmen, who leave their children to the wives, who in turn hand them over to the maids while they spend their husband's money. No one is going to give you medals for your honesty."

That Yuletide, Commando threw a Santa party at the Basti. He used the grounds of the Pyramid School. All were invited including Mr. and Mrs. Gomes. They thought it discreet to attend.

A tall casuarina tree was propped up by bricks and stones on the open air stage. Electric lights twinkled through the gray-green needles and there were strips of cotton, lots of cotton, on the branches, symbolizing snow. Not a single slum child had ever seen or felt snow in their tender little lives!

"My brothers and sisters! Today we celebrate the Festival of Giving. Santa was a wonderful Punjabi Saint, who decided to renounce life and take up 'sanyas.' He gave all his worldly belongings to people like us. Each year we shall celebrate this day. Now Santa will distribute your gifts." Commando stepped off the podium and propelled a man with a huge sack, red clothes and a snow white beard, towards the waiting crowd. He had requested Gomes to put on the rented robes, as he was the most familiar with Yuletide celebrations. Stainless steel utensils, sheets, shawls, sweets and potato chips were distributed to the crowds. Commando had paid for them. The Festival of Giving was celebrated every year thereafter. Many more children from Naya Gaon joined St. Phillips and were given a good education. Mrs. Goel resigned, citing health issues. She joined the staff of the Pyramid School, where the culture was more to her liking. Occasional corporal punishment was acceptable and the work was by rote, not encouraged by thinking or questioning.

The Gomes-Commando friendship blossomed. It gave Renuka great pleasure to talk to Belinda Maria, whenever they went over for a meal to Commando's Palace. Both women had the mannerisms and 'nakhras' of convent educated girls. Both conversed in faultless English. Bindiya's admission at St. Phillips was an eagerly awaited event, but as she was only two and a half years old and too young for school, the Gomes' and Commandos' went about cementing their own friendship. It appeared as if there never had been any acrimony. The Basti parents brought 'sifaarishes' or recommendations to Commando and Renuka. These were passed on to Gomes. Unless a child was severely impaired, she was never refused a seat at St, Phillips.

- -

The milkman stood at Belinda's door. "Give me my money! You did not pay me last month either."

"I'm coming." Belinda went in and returned within a few minutes. She stood before the man with a bucket of water. "Take this water and here are sixty rupees."

"Why are you giving me water? Is this a joke?" The milkman grabbed the money, counted it and tipped the bucket of water onto the road. "You owe me a hundred and twenty more. Go and bring it. I am in a hurry."

Belinda stood her ground. "The water is in exchange for the water you mixed. The money is for the milk."

The man towered over her. "Bring me my money, or else..." He threatened.

"Or else what?"

"I shall sort you out."

Belinda whistled and her Cocker Spaniel, Stella, shot out of the house. "Catch!" she commanded. The milkman ran with the dog tearing his dhoti whenever she got a chance.

Commando laughed when Gomes narrated the story. "Large man with gold earrings and a huge wart on his nose?"

Belinda nodded. "I've no milkman delivering milk now. They are boycotting our home."

"Leave it to me," smiled Commando.

The next day the same milkman arrived with two kilos of the purest milk. The earrings were missing, but the ear lobes were stitched after gashes caused by their unceremonious removal.

"I don't know how he does it, but he is a God-send." Belinda told Gomes.

"Its best we don't ask," her husband countered. "He has his methods and they work. The less we know the better."

By "joining the enemy" life became far more comfortable for the Gomes.' Commando sent across three artisans to repair their roof which leaked during the monsoon. Their pleas before the Governing Board had fallen on deaf ears. No money was exchanged. It was Commando's way of thanking them for giving him the respectability he craved. The day Gomes bought a small, second-hand car at a discounted price, Commando sent asbestos sheets and angle irons towards the construction of a temporary garage. "Nothing fancy," he assured them. It was a simple structure with a roof over four irons. "Nobody will steal your car," he promised Belinda when she asked for walls and a door. "You have Commando's word for it."

At the school Annual Day, Principal Gomes handed out ten scholarships for deserving chidren. Ravi and Vijay won them from their respective classes. The Scholarship Fund was instituted by Commando.

By the next semester, Vijay's jauntiness increased and his work took a dive. He began back-chatting the teachers and stealing the other children's food, just for a lark. He often said, "I am Commando! If you do not listen to me I shall sort you out." Ravi tried to dissuade him but to no avail.

Gomes brought the matter up with Commando. He felt it was his duty towards a friend. A year earlier he would have trembled at the idea. The Chacha heard him out and said he would tackle his nephew.

Vijay was tied across a chair, his bottom exposed. All doors were bolted, the curtains drawn. Commando stood over him with a flexible willow switch. Not a word was exchanged as the rod hissed through the air onto the child's backside. Vijay clenched his teeth and closed his eyes. He did not cry.

Commando untied him and said, "Don't ever do anything I would not approve of. When you learn the ways of the world and can distinguish right from wrong, you will have earned the right to make your own rules. Till then do not touch anyone's things or talk back to the teachers. Do I make myself clear?"

Vijay's lip trembled as he nodded.

"I became Commando by looking after people and punishing the bad ones. You will have to prove that you are as good as me. I never got to finish school, but you have the chance. Some day you shall be a bigger Commando than I. Till then you do what you are told, nothing else."

Vijay limped as he walked out of the room. When his mother saw the thin red welts she cried but held her tongue. She had implicit faith in whatever her brother-in-law did.

Vijay worked hard, hoping to become like his beloved Chacha someday.

"Power comes through money and the barrel of a gun." Commando repeated. "Money wins more friends than the truth. But we have to learn the truth first and use it to our advantage. Our personal lives have to be clean, our motives fair. That is the starting point of power. It has to be wielded through cash and the gun."

Renuka shivered as he spoke. Commando could be very intense and obtuse at times.

- -

CHAPTER XII

"What can be more foolish than to think that all this rare fabric of heaven and earth could come by chance, when all the skill of art is not able to make an oyster."— Jeremy Taylor.

AANGANWADI...
THE GOVERNMENT CRECHE

Sonu, the garbage man, threw his son in the air. The child shrieked with delight. He was a beautiful baby, chubby, fair with green-gold eyes. Gulabo looked on indulgently. They now lived in the Mehtas' quarters. Durgi and Hira were back in the Bari Kothi servant lines.

"He looks just like you," Sonu smiled at his wife.

Gulabo looked heaven wards and offered a silent prayer to the gods. "Never let him find out!"

Little Chintu arrived within eight months of their marriage. He was delivered by Durgi, who made it a point to tell the proud father that the child was a month premature.

"Looks healthy enough to me!" said Sonu extending his arms towards the baby.

After her marriage, Gulabo settled down, thankful that she did not have to cater to the Lalajis of the world. When Shaku called her to nurse the twins, she went gladly. Her uncomplicated life with Sonu had pushed aside all rancor and jealousy. Deepak plied her with vitamins and she became strong and energetic.

Meals were provided by the Maalkin according to the Maalik's dietary recommendations. After all her milk had to be rich enough for young Memsahib's twins. As Durgi was back to cooking for the Baksh household, food for Chintu and Sonu was never in short supply.

When Mustapha, Shaku and Hakim went to Afghanistan, the twins had been weaned for over two years.

Gulabo continued looking after them. Chintu played with them and Shaku wanted all three to go to the Basti School together. They were still underage. "I'd like them to start at St. Phillips, not the Basti," said Hakim.

He was overruled by his wife and father-in-law. Both felt that the children had to begin at the grass root level of Indian society.

Amina Bi handed Gulabo a plastic box of sevian kheer. "It is Id. I made enough for everyone. Take it home for your family."

Gulabo thanked the old woman. "You are very good to me Ammiji."

Amina Bi smiled. She remembered a fire brand that had caused so much trouble. Motherhood suited the child.

Mustapha still had reservations about Gulabo. He had not forgotten the tongue-lashing Durgi meted out before leaving the Bari Kothi. "A leopard never changes it's spots!" he murmured.

- -

Khamo landed at the Bari Kothi one morning, son in tow and hugely pregnant. She had a black eye and a bandaged leg. "I have come to stay," she announced. "Burfu's papa beats me a lot and has brought home a 'soutan,' a mistress." She referred to Ramu whose name she could not use as per the custom. He was the 'wimp' rejected by Gulabo and passed onto her half sister. The 'soutan' was a village woman who decided she liked Ramu and wanted to live with him. Maamu, Durgi's brother and Ramu's father approved of the arrangement because he considered Khamo lazy as she was reluctant to work in the fields. They were subsistence farmers and could not hire labour for the work. Often women pulled the plough if bulls were not available. The daughters-in-law were supposed to dig, sow and water after completing their household chores. Khamo, a city girl, refused to do so. When Banti offered her services, provided she could move in with Ramu, Khamo was given the option to leave for her paternal home.

Durgi was beside herself with anger. "How can you come here? Once a daughter is given away, there is no place for her in her father's home. We paid good dowry for you. How could Maamu send you here?"

"Well he did and Burfu's father has brought home another woman. Best of luck to them!"

"What happened to your eye?" Durgi asked.

"Banti hit me! She is as strong as an ox and as ugly too! I cannot and will not work in the fields. The sun is too strong, the soil too hard. I am a city girl and cannot do all this."

"City girl?" spat out Durgi. "Then you better change into a village girl and go back. We have enough mouths to feed without you and your son. And I see another child on the way. What do you think this is... an orphanage?"

As usual, Hira brought in some semblance of order in what was turning into a cat fight. "Woman! Can't you see she has a sore leg? How can she go back unless it is healed? The Maalik will medicate her. Let the child be born and I shall personally take her back to her Maamu."

It turned out that there were daily fights ever since Banti moved in. She poured hot oil on Khamo's leg and threatened to kill her son. Durgi's daughter was frightened enough to run away.

Deepak did start a course of treatment. The leg had been neglected and was oozing pus.

"What did you use on this?" he asked.

"Dough mixed with turmeric powder, but it just got worse. Then I was sent to the field and slipped in the slush."

Deepak shook his head in dismay. "Must be paining a lot?"

"Yes it does but who has any time for pain? Hard work makes one forget everything and unkind in-laws treat the cows better."

"Well your mother will look after you." He handed her samples of antibiotics and pain killers. Deepak kept a stash of these. They were left by salesmen from pharmaceutical companies and came in handy for his very destitute patients, who could not afford consultation fees or medication.

Khamo kept quiet. She knew he would not understand how poverty created its own tough rules. She was not welcome in her own home.

Gulabo was wary of her half-sister, who had aged and become very bitter. She recalled the fights they used to have and the abuse Khamo hurled at her. She was sure that within a few days the same patterns would emerge. Chintu and Burfu got on well. They played a lot, shared their food and bathed together with the warm water that sloshed out of the Persian wheel cans.

"Obviously life has been good to you!" Khamo's observation was more of an accusation than a compliment.

"Sonu is a good man. And I have a beautiful child."

"And I got the left-overs! You hated Ramu, and were right to do so. But you all pushed me into marrying him. Life for me would have been better in the city."

"It is 'kismet,' our destiny," countered Gulabo. "Life is the fruit of our Karma. The gods will look after you."

"Don't give me your fraudulent religious ideas! You were born on the wrong side of the blanket and were blessed with everything good. Your Karma should have dictated otherwise. Why am I being punished instead?"

Gulabo moved away and went inside to meet Durgi. She knew when to quit the battle field.

Khamo held her aching stomach and doubled up. The antibiotics caused nausea and her intestines were on fire. She rushed to the latrine every few minutes. Yes, there were latrines in the Bari Kothi servant lines. Due to the shortage of piped municipal water, these were dry latrines, but they were convenient.

"I won't have the Maalik's medicine," Khamo told her mother. Durgi asked Deepak to persuade her daughter otherwise. Being the kind man he was, he refused to force the issue. Hira called the local leech man. He strolled in with a cloth bag that held many plastic containers with small holes in the lids for air. "Cheesa Cheese," said the labels on the boxes. The man peered into each, and finally chose one with thin, thread like leeches. The other boxes had worms of various sizes depending on when they had fed. He placed twenty of these around the wound on Khamo's leg. They attached themselves to the frayed flesh and started sucking. Within an hour they had ballooned out like large, purple grapes. The man allowed them to fall off before storing them in the plastic box. He smoked, chatted and drank tea while he waited. Clamping the lid on, he murmured, "There, there my beauties! You have had enough for a week! Give me a hundred," he told Hira.

"We are poor people. We cannot afford a hundred."

"I am making this concession only for you!" he said, wagging a finger in Hira's face. He did not want to lose out on a new customer. With the inroads made by modern medicine, the demand for leeches was almost non-existent in the towns. "Give me ninety."

He settled for seventy-five and promised to return in four days to complete the treatment. Surprisingly the wound healed, leaving just a pitted scar on an otherwise healthy limb.

Deepak examined the leg. He was pleasantly surprised. India's rich but forgotten traditions never ceased to amaze him.

Durgi approached Deepak for a job for Khamo. It was the oft repeated story of grinding poverty and not enough earning power to climb out of it. Pushpa refused to add another person to the retinue in the house. Besides, another hungry mouth stealing the rations, was just not feasible.

"Train her for your clinic," Durgi begged.

"Let me think about it," said Deepak.

In the end it was a chance meeting with the Deputy Commissioner, that decided Khamo's future job prospects. "We have an NGO called the Aanganwadi Project.

Volunteers are given an honorarium of Rs 600 per month, to look after children from the Bastis. They educate these children and cook a midday meal for them. It is one of the best projects created by the government for the poorest of poor. I'll call the people in charge tomorrow and she will be enrolled. It's always a pleasure to help you and yours, Doctor!" Deepak knew he would have to return the favour some day. He personally drove Khamo for the interview.

The Aanganwadi is a beautiful dream of a group of concerned people, for the benefit of destitute India. Sweepers, beggars, rickshaw pullers, maids, boot-polishers, drivers, peons and many other below-the-poverty-line candidates, can go about their jobs, leaving their children in the care of the local Aanganwadi. Any venue is considered a good location, as long as it is at the epicenter of the families concerned. Not a paisa is charged from the parents. Each group of twenty-five children is assigned to a teacher and a helper. Khamo was to help the teacher and cook the midday meal from the three given options: dry milk, sugar and rice, combined into kheer; flour, oil and sugar for rounded 'pinnies' or a sweet, cracked-wheat porridge called 'daliya.' In a typical five hour working day, the helper spent most of her time making the nutritious puddings. This is given the euphemism "mid-day meal."

The cooking vessel was huge, the gas ring small. Therefore the preparation took at least three hours. When and if the teacher was called out, the helper substituted, unable to make time for the puddings.

"So she goes out often?" asked Durgi about the Aanganwadi teacher, her mind probing the immense possibilities of this bit of information.

"Three days a week she's out either delivering registers or bringing them back. She also goes with reports and bills and to attend training programmes."

"Who looks after the children then?"

"I do!" said Khamo with great pride.

"On those three days, you'd better bring some rations home," Durgi ordered her daughter.

"I can't do that! Suppose I get caught?"

"Well... see to it you aren't! We need every spoonful we can get. I am looking after your two children, so this is the least you can do. And don't forget to hand in your salary to me." The mother left Khamo no option at all. No one disobeyed Durgi. Besides, with the arrival of the baby girl, two months earlier, Khamo was afraid her mother would send her back to Maamu.

And so the Aanganwadi children, "age zero to six," lost out on quantity while 'Auntyji' waddled home, weighed down by bags of rations tied to her waist and stitched into her voluminous salwar.

"Where is Bimla today?" the 'inspectress' – for that was her official designation- asked Khamo.

"She has gone to the post office to collect the monthly rations." The government had chosen the nearest Post Office as a convenient distribution point.

"How late are the rations?"

"We did not have any for the past fifteen days."

"Show me the stock registers."

"Bimla has them, not I."

"Well tell Bimla to get them ready for inspection by tomorrow. I shall be back in the morning."

The inspectress walked into the first room crammed with children. She wrinkled her nose. "What is that smell? Why are the windows closed?"

"It is very cold and the children wet their clothes. I try to keep them warm by closing all windows."

"You talk too much! You are supposed to take the children out to do their jobs."

"But Madamji, then who will sit with the rest of the children? Some of them are zero years old."

"You find a way. I am not supposed to go into those details."

"We are supposed to have another helper. There are too many children in one room," Khamo pointed out.

The inspectress looked embarrassed. "I know, I know!" she said testily. "It is hard to find volunteers for the Aanganwadi."

Of course thought Khamo. Only a lunatic or a starving person would take on the thankless task.

True to her word, the inspectress was back next morning. Bimla and Khamo stood at attention as the woman sat on a chair, pouring over records, bills and registers. Khamo scratched her head, squashing a louse.

"You are obviously new here!" screamed the inspectress. "Stand at attention. You are distracting me. I have five more centers to inspect today. Yours is the first. This register shows that your stocks should still be lasting. Whatever you measure for sixty children every day amounts to five kilos of rice, two of sugar and five large mugs of dry milk. Multiply it by 27 days of the month, excluding Sundays. Your dry stocks should take you into next month. Bimla, tell me why the rations have finished so soon and why did you ask for a fresh supply?"

Bimla, who was a petite woman with a lackluster personality, worsened by a husband and mother-in-law who regularly beat her, was shivering and completely tongue-tied. When she found her voice, she said, "I don't know Madamji. Khamo told me the rations were over and I sent in the requisition slip."

"But you did fill the 'in and out' stock register?"

"She told me what to write every day."

"Who's in charge here, you or the helper?"

"I am Madamji," said Bimla, sniffling into her dupatta.

In the end the truth was out. A month's supply of rations had been purloined and neither woman admitted taking them.

"I shall be back at four in the afternoon. If the rations are not here by then, you both will lose your jobs."

Bimla, her conscience clear and spirit retrieved, shouted at Khamo, "You'd better do something about this you bitch! Otherwise I shall tell her. You need not think I did not suspect what is going on!" Bimla tried to get back some of her lost authority.

Khamo went home and asked Durgi for the first month's salary she had handed over to her the week before. Hira took her in the rickshaw, to the 'mandi,' where they bought a month's supply of rations. When the inspectress arrived at four in the afternoon, carrying a weighing scale, the rations were measured to the last gram and placed under lock and key. Khamo did not steal for many months to come and Durgi's complaints grew longer and louder.

By Diwali, Durgi had accepted the fact that Khamo and the children were back permanently. Hira was his daughter's silent accomplice and conspirator.

Sonu, Gulabo, Chintu, Khamo and her two children arrived at the Bari Kothi for 'Diwali,' the Festival of Lights. 'Diyas,' tiny earthen bowls, overflowing with mustard oil and fat, worm like cotton wicks, were lit on every wall and along the garden path-ways. Durgi put on each light in the bungalow and opened the windows. This was the day the goddess of wealth, Lakshmi entered the homes of her devotees. Deepak, Pushpa, Mustapha, Amina Bi, Hakim and Shaku sat on the carpet, in the sitting room, gambling at cards. Lakshmi liked money games on the festival dedicated to her.

Hira and Sonu were in charge of the fireworks. They took the children onto the lawn and lit rockets, bombs, sparklers, catherine wheels and pomegranate shaped 'anars.' No one even thought of the numerous children who lost their lives every year, preparing the fireworks in ill equipped factories that followed no safety rules whatsoever. The only criterion for getting a job in such a factory was a tiny hand that could stuff dynamite into small containers. That the same hand could light a match in forbidden anticipation of an exciting bang, was not considered. Entire factories blew up in this fashion and a few lines in the newspaper were devoted to the "charred beyond recognition bodies of a number of children." Cases were filed against the owner of the factory. He would grease the right palms and incriminating police files would be "lost" by next Diwali. The children were India's collateral damage, forgotten by the turn of the page on which their deaths were reported. There was so much horror amongst the destitute that the well to do developed a thick skin to avoid thinking of it.

The Baksh's budgeted Rs 10000 for the annual festival. Gifts were exchanged, new clothes bought and sweets distributed. Till midnight, the country resounded with loud bangs and the sky was lit up with fairy lights from giant sparklers. It was reminiscent of a country at war. By midnight, all but a few diyas were out; the crackers exploded and finished; the sweets eaten. Gulabo and her family went back to the Mehta home. Khamo and her babies lay on the mud floor of Durgi's spare room, covered under light blankets against the chill of a new day. "I wish Bapu was here today," Burfu whispered to his mother. "It was such a nice tamasha... don't you think so Ma?"

Khamo had nothing to say and suckled her daughter in silence. Not able to steal rations from the Aanganwadi, she tried to work out a strategy to earn more money. If she did not come up with a solution soon, Durgi would personally take her back to Maamu, of that she had no doubt. She would consult Gulabo in the morning. After all her half sister had managed to earn something even before her marriage to Sonu.

"It's easy," said Gulabo. "It's the best way to make money if you don't worry about what people say. All men want it and we have it. But you will have to look better. I shall take you to Maya's Beauty Parlour for a make-over."

"Are you still into the dhanda?"

"Do I need to? Chintu's papa is into big money now. We sell broken fridges and furniture too. I work at the Mehta's for the free quarter. I don't really need to work at all."

"India is amazing!" Commando made this observation to his wife. "We waste nothing at all. Men have grown rich selling plastic bags, bottles, bits of iron, old furniture, clothes, broken utensils and cardboard. Do you remember Sonu the garbage man? He came to me for a loan."

"For what?" asked Renuka.

"He is opening a kabaadi shop near Madamji's Basti School. It is good to see one of our kind making it big."

"Has he made it big? And who are your kind?"

"You definitely are!" said Commando. "But seriously! I can never forget my roots. Nor will my family let me. By God's grace, I have done well. That is because we have never taken away anyone's livelihood. 'Pet par laat marne se Bhagwan bhi tyaag deta hai.' If you take away a man's livelihood, God too shall desert you."

"Waste Management!" murmured Renuka.

"Whats that," he asked.

"It is a subject offered at the University. Our kabaadi-wallahs could give them a lecture or two."

Maya's Parlour did a good job on Khamo. They trimmed, ironed and streaked her waist length hair. They painted her nails, steamed and scoured her face and taught her how to apply makeup. Gulabo handed over some of her own discarded outfits. When Khamo lined up at the Lalaji's sweet shop, she was noticed by one of his touts and led up stairs. Munni Bai had found the perfect method to cater to her husband's insatiable sexual appetite. She even started advising her friends on how to live in harmony with a happy husband, provided he handed over all his worldly possessions into the right hands.

The Lala was fatter than ever before. He was unable to put any effort into love-making and left it all to Khamo. She had been tutored well by Gulabo. As she worked on him she thought, "This is so much easier than the Aanganwadi! I shall keep that for the respectability it affords. My children need that. Let's see how much I can get out of this impotent stud."

When the Lala handed her a crisp hundred rupee note, arranged for by Munni Bai, Khamo returned it saying, "Inflation is up and I have to keep myself beautiful for you."

Lalaji shouted at no one in particular, "Oye, bring me 25 more!"

An urchin, who had been watching proceedings through the key hole, rushed down stairs and brought the requisite amount.

"You look so familiar!" said Lala Bharat Kumar. "There was this beautiful girl once. She had green eyes. She smelt like you and wore almost the same kind of clothes. I wonder where she is now?"

Khamo smiled. Gulabo had not told her about the Lala. She went home and handed Durgi a hundred rupees. She hid the extra twenty five.

The inspectress paid another visit to the Naya Gaon Aanganwadi. She found Bimla missing. "Where is she now?" she asked Khamo.

"She is on a two week training programme."

"Are you stealing rations?"

"God forbid!" Khamo caught her ear lobes like a penitent child and sat on the floor.

"Get up you fool! I am a kind woman. Because of my kindness you did not lose your job." She got up to leave as the helper touched her feet in gratitude.

Khamo saw the inspectress back to her jeep. When she re-entered the Aanganwadi, a year old bawled continously, screaming, "Ma! Ma! Ma!" calling out for his mother who had gone to clean the toilets at Commando's Palace. Khamo hit him across the mouth. "Keep quiet!" she hissed. The child screamed harder. She went on hitting him till he became quiet and lay down sobbing softly, thumb in his mouth. Khamo smiled to herself. She had trained many children in the same fashion. Her class was the quietest, most subdued, on the block.

Bimla returned with a load of drawing books. She showed everyone the origami creations, collages, pencil shaving flowers, leaf and feather collections and ice-cream-stick puppets, she had learnt to make. The training camp had taught her a lot but the authorities failed to provide a stock of pencils, paper, crayons or story books for the children. They still got their mid-day meal and then lay down to sleep, quietly, without making a sound for fear of being thrashed. They were well trained.

"Where do the materials go?" a concerned visitor enquired.

"They are not sent from the head office."

"Have you lodged a complaint?"

"Many times," Bimla rolled her eyes in mock dismay. "They take no notice."

Some pencils and copy books, super scribed with the Aanganwadi logo, were found at the Pyramid School. An enquiry was instituted. The Aanganwadi committee called witnesses. Bimla and Khamo went to depose together with the Pyramid School coordinator. Everyone was tight lipped and provided no clues. In the end the tabled report was inconclusive. As usual more time was spent covering up tracks and telling "truthful" lies, than bringing corruption to an end. "Poverty makes us line our pockets so that our children may eat. We do not bite the hand that feeds us," said Khamo with immense satisfaction.

Sunday found the two half sisters sitting under Gulabo's neem tree, by the side of the road. This was where Sonu had re-entered her life. The children were playing near the well at the Bari Kothi.

It was a quiet, private moment.

"So you went to the Lalaji at the sweet shop?" Khamo asked.

Gulabo whipped around, startled. "Who told you?"

"No one, just something the fat man said."

"Did he talk to you about the child?"

As soon as the words left her lips, Gulabo realized that her sister did not know about Chintu and that she had given herself away. "Please do not tell Chintu's father. Ma and Bapu have kept my secret... you must too."

"Of course I will. You have nothing to worry about." Khamo realized she had yet another stick for the future.

The future came knocking on Khamo's door, earlier than expected.

Chintu and Burfu fought over a guava given by Shaku. Chintu bit off a larger piece and his cousin went crying to the mother. Khamo had had a bad day at the Aanganwadi where the inspectress, on a surprise visit, caught her thrashing the weeping infants into submission.

"Is this how you treat tender lives? What kind of people will these infants become? They will have lost their tongues, their curiosity, their playfulness!"

Her assistant tried to calm her down. "Madamji, she is only disciplining them the way we discipline our own children," she reasoned.

"If this is how you treat your own kids, God save them!" shouted the inspectress. She turned towards Khamo and warned her, "This is your second offence. I shall personally throw you out if I catch you doing something wrong again. Be warned!"

Khamo, who had a splitting headache, slapped Chintu. "You better learn to share everything with my son. Do you hear me?"

Gulabo came running to see why her son was crying. "You had no business to hit my child! Burfu is equally naughty but I never hit him. After all that I have done for you and your family, is this how you repay us?"

Khamo had enough of yelling. Her head throbbed. She said wearily, "You have given me your leftovers, nothing more... so shut your mouth!"

Sonu, home for lunch, walked into the middle of a slanging match. He held Chintu in his lap, wiped away the tears and told Khamo quietly, "She is right... you cannot hit my son. Talk to us instead."

Khamo exploded. "Your son? Did you say your son? Do you want to know who's child this is? You poor fool!" She stomped out of the room, carrying Burfu in her arms.

A secret, kept so by three people, was out in the open. Sonu put the child down. He said nothing, did his work, returned home for meals. He would not talk to Gulabo who felt he would do something dreadful. A very deep love was being tested and their usually cheerful lives were shattered by a careless remark. Chintu clung to the only father he knew, who held him but never spoke or smiled. Khamo stopped visiting her half sister at the Mehtas.

- -

Sonu and Gulabo tried to work things out. The couple would often walk out to the park, sitting under the silk-cotton trees. Gulabo explained the circumstances to her beloved husband. He listened but grew to hate Durgi more and more, as he identified her with all that had gone wrong. As for Hira, he was too timid to be blamed for anything.

Chintu would often wipe the tears from his mother's cheeks and beg her to smile. Sometimes he'd put his head in Sonu's lap and go to sleep. Sonu would always hold him tight.

"I've been a haramzaadi all my life. No one let me forget the stigma of illegitimacy... ever! I coped with it the best way I could, but I don't want Chintu to suffer what I went through. No one knows at the school, but one day, my sister will fling it in my face again. She is jealous of our peaceful, comfortable lives. What can we do for this child?"

- -

It was Mrs. Mehta who heard Chintu crying. Gulabo had not reported for work and the old lady wanted to know why. A kabaadi-wallah walked in and said that Sonu had not gone to the shop. The police found two bodies, a man and a woman, hanging from the neem tree by the roadside. Even in death they held hands and no one could open the clasp without grievous injury to the fingers.

Durgi held her grandson and sobbed inconsolably into his hair, "Why would they do such a thing? She was so beautiful and now there is nothing. They were doing so well and were happy."

The same question was on everyone's lips. Deepak offered to get a post-mortem done. Hira would not hear of it. Shaku wanted to put Chintu into the Basti School but Commando had other plans.

As Pushpa held the infant and put an arm around Durgi's shoulders, the grandmother said, "They have left so much for this child! There is a shop, three workers, so much 'maal,' stuff, yet to be sold. Gulabo's father will have to look after it all."

"Did Sonu have any relatives?" Shaku enquired.

"None but us. He was a good man." Chintu was bewildered and did not know what had occurred. He cried and waited for his parents to come home. By their suicide, they closed an ugly chapter, and cleared the way for Chintu's unblemished future. Within a year, everyone would forget the haramzaadi and her rag-man lover. Two decades later, Chintu would advertise in the dailies, asking for household goods that could be recycled. He would go from home to home in a mini-truck, buying goods discarded by owners. Some day he would be the proud owner, the Maalik of an antique shop that sold salvaged, refurbished goods at exorbitant prices.

No police report was filed. Durgi and Hira said the children were depressed for some unknown reason. Khamo, who knew the whole story, kept quiet. She left the Aanganwadi and moved into Gulabo's quarter to work for the Mehtas. Her customers now had an 'adda' or permanent point to come to, and she still visited the sweet shop thrice a week. When she asked the Mehtas for another room, they gladly agreed to build one on the condition that she would share fifty percent of the cost. Khamo, a wealthy woman in her own right, promptly agreed.

"Unrequited love," said some. "An extra marital affair," reported others. No one really understood why a young couple, who had worked so hard for their place in the sun, would commit suicide. That they had done so was the only reality. The moment it was dubbed "a suicide pact" by the coroner, the police lost interest. They had too much on their plate without suicides being thrown in too. "Two less people in an overcrowded city. That makes two less probable crimes from the slum. I am thankful!" declared the thanedar for whom Gulabo and Sonu were mere statistics.

"I wonder what went wrong?" Commando discussed Sonu's death with his wife. "He was doing well and they seemed a happy couple; an unusual marital state in most of the Basti. He had even paid back the loan. Sometimes life is lost through our ill starred destinies."

"What about the child?" asked Renuka, whose common sense never failed her.

"Gomes has promised to admit him at St. Phillips. Remember how much trouble we had with him, till Belinda and you met?"

"I think you sorted out the Board before that," she responded.

"I sorted out the minister, not the Board you silly woman!" Commando chucked his wife under the chin. "The board members are small fry. The minister is the crooked one. He accepts bribes and flaunts rules. One woman's misery is another woman's gateway into a comfortable future. I believe Khamo has a two room set up and is doing rather well," said Commando who kept his ear to the ground.

"How do you know so much?" his wife asked.

"It is my business to know! Information, however slight, keeps me alive and ahead." Renuka shuddered. She knew so little about Commando's work. It was frightening at times.

- -

CHAPTER XIII

"Where two discourse, if the anger of one rises, he
is the wise man who lets the contest fall."... Plutarch

THE DINNER

Gulabo and Sonu's deaths were a distant nightmare. Chintu settled down well at St. Phillips. His cousin Burfu joined the School too. Hira bought a second hand scooter to drop his grandsons at St. Phillips. He also used it to get the kabaadi business done. He still had the rickshaw and took his family for occasional rides to the park, created by Commando for the people of the Basti. On hot summer days, the open spaces and fountains offered a breath of moist, cool air. The children used the swings, slides, jungle gyms and brick dolls houses. Durgi still worked at the Bari Kothi, on an enhanced salary and had an assistant to help her.

"Lazy good for nothing girl!" she grumbled to Amina Bi. "I cannot trust a single piece of the dairy maid dinner set to her. She will break it."

Amina Bi smiled and soothed her, paying an indirect compliment, "Only you and I can wash that Durgi. No one else can. But you are not getting younger and can use her help. Why don't you train her in the ways of the Bari Kothi?"

The twins rushed in. Both were at St. Phillips but in different sections. The teachers said they could not cope with them when they were together.

"Didi!" said Khush. "Give me a sweet french toast. My friends are waiting and I have to go and play. Be quick about it!"

"My lovely Dadi," pleaded Luv. "Make me a cheese toast the way I like it. Didi can't do it that well!"

The two women laughed and started preparations. "Why can they not choose the same thing?" said Durgi.

"See how sharp Luv is. She can wheedle anything out of me. A typical girl!" She was proud of her grand-daughter.

"God's greatest blessing is not to give us fools for children," said Durgi. "I feel sorry for my brother. My Ruby married his youngest son and has the dullest children possible. When I went to the village for their third child's first Lohri, I found the elder children so stupid and slow."

"Maybe the effect of the village... education makes such a difference. Khamo's son seems bright enough."

"You could be right. The city is a jungle. We have to be sharp here to survive." Durgi agreed. "The village moves at a slower pace, but none of us can flaunt the rules made by the elders. The village Panchayat is all powerful. Ruby's friend finished her schooling and fell in love with a shop keeper's son. The elders warned her not to marry him as he was of a higher caste. They paid no heed."

"Then what happened?" asked Amina Bi as she flipped over the cheese toast.

"They ran away and got married at a temple in Dera Bassi. The Panchayat told the parents of both parties to deal with the situation or else.... They sent out a posse who kidnapped them from their two room apartment in Ludhiana and brought them home. Both were strangulated by the uncles and brothers, their bodies placed before the Panchayat Ghar. The Khap had decreed it so."

Amina Bi shuddered. "How could they do it? And what is a Khap?"

"Its members make and pass laws in the village. Nobody dare flout them. They are the village judiciary. The police is considered State machinery. When the constables came to arrest them, they showed no remorse whatsoever. The mother was particularly hard hearted and said her daughter needed to be finished off for family honour's sake. Sixteen people are in jail today- the girl's parents and brothers included. The case is still going on."

When the twins came in to take their toasts, they wondered why the women were not smiling.

"I want to take Abba and Ammi to Afghanistan for a visit. Abba made this promise to her a long time back. It is for me to fulfill it. You should stay here with the children." Hakim told Shaku.

"We were to take the children too. Why have you changed your mind? They are old enough now."

"The Taliban is regrouping. Kabul seems the only safe place. Abba insists on going to meet his family, before it is too late."

The old couple were active but getting feebler. Hakim wanted to make their last wishes come true.

"Then I shall go too. I made a promise to Aziza. God knows I am five years too late!"

"Late for what?"

"To start a girls school at Khas."

"I don't think any of you ought to go." Deepak said while they were seated on the carpet, eating dinner at the annexe. "Reports are not good from Afghanistan. The USA has no control over areas outside Kabul. The President lives in a well fortified palace. He would not last a day without American protection."

"I know," agreed Hakim. "But we are Pathans of the same faith. They will not harm us."

"What about Shaku?" Pushpa asked.

"I will be wearing a burkha," laughed Shaku. "No one will know who I am."

When Commando came to the Basti School to make a small donation, Shaku brought up the topic of their trip. He too had heard of the unrest in Afghanistan, a country that survived on its poppy fields, because the promised American aid was routed elsewhere, and because all the usual sources of income had dried up due to an unending war. Heroin was brought to India from Afghanistan and his couriers picked it up on the LOC or Line of Control. From there it was transported by sea, land and air to all parts of the country and other continents too. Commando had never travelled into Afghanistan but had trusted men across the border in Pakistan, where he supplied IEDs in bulk.

"I think Madamji, you ought not to go. Your father has given the right suggestion."

To Shaku, challenges were like ambrosia. They made her adrenaline rush and she had to take them on. She was determined to make the trip.

"Bhaiya, you have protected this Basti for years. I am sure you can protect me and mine anywhere, even outside India."

Commando beamed with pride. The compliment was huge and paid by one of the most educated, intelligent women he had ever had the pleasure of meeting. "Of course I can. I have people all over. You make the trip Madamji and I shall bring you back safe into your parents' arms."

Shaku mentioned Commando's promise to the family.

Deepak was not impressed. "How can one man have such power? If he did, he would be a cabinet minister by now."

"Baba you don't understand!" Shaku was impatient. "Cabinet ministers are mere puppets. Commando has real power. He is the biggest man here. He does not have an official designation but wields immense clout. Even the so called ministers come to him for help. Hakim and I have met the most senior officials at his home. Not a man can sneeze without Commando's permission."

"Don't be dramatic child. If so, why have I not heard of him?"

"Why do you think your clinic is running so smoothly? Has the police ever tapped you for money for chai-pani or hafta? Has the Municipal Committee ever tried to point out the 'illegalities' of your clinic? Have the goons of Jullundur ever tried to intimidate you for cash? Look around you. False cases are being slapped on against others just to line pockets. Dr. Prasad had to fork out two lakhs because an Estate Office Junior Engineer, changed his blue prints and showed that the hospital wall had swallowed six inches extra land. Six inches Baba! It is because Commando protects us. You have not heard of him in your sanitized world because he chooses to keep a low profile. He has a huge house, guarded by a dozen loyalists. He invites all the bureaucracy and gets jobs done. The Basti worships him!"

"Is this true?" Deepak addressed the question to his son-in-law, a man whose judgment he trusted implicitly.

"I am afraid so. We, as Muslims, have been protected by him. He follows no religion and has his own set of rules. How he does it we do not know. Where does he get the resources from? That too we do not know. But his people are all over the place, keeping an eye on things."

"I must meet this remarkable young man," said Deepak. "Pushpa, fix a date and let's have Commando over for dinner. Bhabi, you can prepare the best korma and biryani."

And so it came to pass that Commando, Renuka, Bindiya and little Bahadur came for dinner to the Bari Kothi.

- -

"Shall we eat on the carpet or at the table?" Amina Bi asked Pushpa. For if it was to be the traditional Muslim way on the carpet, the annexe needed to be readied.

Pushpa was silent. She asked Deepak who said the Bari Kothi had issued the invitation so it had to be at the table.

Amina Bi was disappointed. "Biryani and korma is best eaten with the hands," she pointed out.

"As he is such a great person, we'd better lay out the dairy maid and silver cutlery for dinner," said Pushpa.

Deepak was shocked on seeing his VIP guest. Commando swaggered in, bravado oozing from every pore. He sported a pony-tail held together by a red elastic band. He wore bell bottomed jeans, frayed at the ends and torn at the knees. A black silk shirt, open till the navel, was contrasted by a red scarf. Every conceivable kind of stone adorned his fingers. Semi-precious stones held by gold chains hung around his sinewy neck. A thick diamond encrusted bracelet encircled his right wrist. He wore the most expensive Rolex watch money could buy. His wife was in a red sari and wore a lot of gold jewelry. The children were in the most garish, sequined cowboy dresses. He was pleased that finally, one of the most well known families in Jullundur had deemed it fit to invite him. He had arrived in society.

"God!" thought Deepak. "Is this peacock the most powerful man in Jullundur?" He wondered how they would get through the evening. He dusted a speck off his black suit and adjusted his red tie. Shaku and Hakim appeared at ease. Pushpa and Amina Bi looked startled. Mustapha was not bothered by anything. Life was too short to worry about disconcerting eccentricities. Besides, he was grateful to meet the man, who Hakim said protected the family.

Commando and Renuka touched everyone's feet. The children did too and were sent to the nursery to play with Luv and Khush, who they knew from St. Phillips. They were served an early meal.

The first surprise was Commando's soft, deep voice. He sat on the sofa, surprisingly at ease with everyone.

The second surprise was Renuka, who spoke faultless English in cultured tones and could hold her own on any subject.

"What name shall I call you?" asked Deepak, a little embarrassed by the moniker given to the man beside him.

"Uncleji, I am Commando," said the man with great humility.

"What do you do Mr.Commando?"

"Uncleji, just 'Commando' will do. I am a trader of sorts. I have many small dhandas. They are too many to list."

"My daughter and son-in-law praise you a lot. They say you do a lot of good work."

"I merely share what I have with others. Those who need help, come to me."

"But what is your source of income?" Deepak asked, still puzzled by the young man's vague replies.

Commando's eyes flashed with anger. "I don't pay taxes, if you must know. Otherwise my wealth and home are for everyone to share. In the slum, our money comes from different sources. It has the same colour as your money but the banks never see it."

Deepak veered off the topic. He realized he had angered his guest by overstepping certain private parameters.

Mustapha, more tuned to the lower rungs of society, assured the young man, "My samdhi means no harm. He just wants to know if you can protect his daughter, and all of us, when we go to Afghanistan later this year."

Commando turned towards the old man. "Abba," he used the more familiar term. "I shall be honest with you all. I know you are worried, given the situation there. My influence extends up to the Pakistan border. I have never been to that country but I do trade with the people there. I have many trusted men across the border. They will protect you all on the trip. You have Commando's word for that."

Deepak caught hold of his hand. "I am sorry I angered a guest in my home, but Shaku is my only child and I worry a lot about her."

Shaku got up and put her arms around her father's shoulders. "Baba it's okay. Commando understands that."

The biryani and korma were a resounding success. Commando ate with his hands and did not use the silver cutlery which Renuka handled so deftly. After they had left, Deepak asked himself, "Pakistan? I'm sure he is into illegal stuff! But isn't everyone today?" He slept well, happy in the belief that Shaku would be safe in Afghanistan.

- -

CHAPTER XIV

"I never could believe that Providence had sent a few men into the world, ready booted and spurred to ride, and millions ready saddled and bridled to be ridden."... Richard Rumbold.

END OF DAYS.

The journey to Afghanistan was no better or worse than the one undertaken so many years earlier. The same rail heads, the same bus rides, the same auto and jeep transfers greeted the group from Jullundur, a town in the Punjab, in North India. The only difference was the presence of Amina Bi. Both Mustapha and she were frailer and needed help boarding trains and vehicles. Mustapha, who was marginally hard of hearing, talked little but often asked for answers to be repeated. He looked forward to meeting his cousins again.

Amina Bi had no contacts to resume. There were no postal addresses, no family names, no friends. She hoped that Afghanistan would throw up clues about a carpet seller who had visited a town called Jullunder, long before India was torn apart into pieces to create two nations of similar people and dissimilar leaders.

Hakim had planned a long holiday. His parents had given him every-thing, asked for nothing. It was payback time and the best he could think of was a holiday in the valley of flowers. The route he planned was through Kashmir, into Gilgit and then to the first town of Afghanistan. He hired the house boat, Taj Mahal, on the Dal Lake for a week. Shaku and he had spent a never-to-be-forgotten honeymoon on it. Bashir's son, Abdullah, took charge of the boat after his father was killed in an encounter with the security forces.

Pots hung from the wooden beams and were ablaze with orange nasturtiums and blood red geraniums. Amina Bi broke a nasturtium pod and smiled as its fresh, astringent taste exploded in her mouth. She plucked a geranium leaf and rubbed it between her fingers, breathing in its strong aroma. "Flowers never look or smell the same in the plains of Punjab," she pointed out to her daughter-in-law. Shaku agreed but her thoughts were with the twins. She wished they had come along too. Now that they had grown up and become more responsive, she missed them more than ever before.

Abdullah escorted the old couple to the bedroom, for they needed to rest after the arduous journey. They lay for a while on thick, soft mattresses, under poly-filled quilts, soothed by the gentle rocking of the boat.

Shaku and Hakim climbed onto the deck above. They held hands and looked into the distance. Mountains surrounded them. The nip of September was turning the poplars gold, the chinar trees a coppery red. Soon the leaves would fall and the lake would be frozen. They were silent. Too many years and memories flashed through their minds. It had been a long and sometimes difficult journey, but together they had travelled it well.

"I asked Abdullah about Bashir. He said the security forces were given a false tip. They stormed the boat but found nothing. As they left, someone... he does not know who... fired from a passing shikaara. The man disappeared but in the panic and crossfire his father was hit in the spine. He died a slow and painful death. He was a good man."

"Yes he was," sighed Shaku. "This is no longer the valley of flowers. They call it the vale of tears now."

"It's not that bad," Hakim teased her. "Not very long ago, we could not visit Kashmir for fear of the militants. We are on the Taj Mahal today, with my parents. That certainly shows a return to normal life."

Shaku shook her head. She had seen too many soldiers behind sand bags and bunkers, all along the route to Srinagar. They marched through the streets, frisked passengers, talked little and kept a sharp eye on every moving object. At check points they held mirrors under cars, opened boots and looked into dash boards. They even rummaged through ladies hand bags and luggage. If this was a normal way of life, what must it have been when the militants ruled? It was hard to imagine and very frightening. The present seemed fleeting and fugacious.

Abdullah served them the perfect meal. His wife had prepared gushtaba with fluffy boiled rice, followed by a lamb biryani and onion raita. Zakir, his fifteen year old son helped carry in the dishes. He was a handsome lad but somewhat sullen and unsmiling. Mustapha asked Abdullah what ailed him. "Nothing! Just teenage blues and the desire to become a hero." The boy hurried down to the kitchen where his mother was heating the saffron and rice kheer.

Hakim and his family spent seven days doing touristy excursions around Srinagar and the surrounding areas. All through their stay, each one felt that silent eyes watched over them. Shaku was sure that Commando's contacts surrounded them. The thought comforted her.

They took the house boat's shikaara and crossed the lake to see the old Mughal gardens, lit up now for night viewing. They bought flowers and fruit from boats that did door to door sales. Amina bought a small sack of dry apricots for Pushpa at half the rate at which they were available at stores in Jullundur. Shaku bought a similar sack of green almonds for Deepak. Mustapha smelled the saffron and settled for a minute quantity of the kind that made him sneeze, for that was the acid test of purity.

Abdullah took them through narrow, kutcha lanes, to visit a carpet factory. Rahim, the owner showed them ancient Persian pieces, hanging from the walls. They looked like velvet but the tiny knots, counted from the reverse, dictated their value. Rahim gingerly lifted an arm on which was draped a gold and blue masterpiece. "We only copy the design from this one. We cannot reproduce these knots. They are too fine and a carpet like this would take years in the making. No one would give the price we'd ask for."

He pointed out the different flowers of Kashmir, woven into the carpet. A poppy here, a rose there and a saffron lily in the corner. Even stylized peacocks, pheasants, wood peckers and parrots made their appearance on the rugs. Shaku, who had never paid much attention to the carpets at home, realized that each design had its own tale to tell.

"Burly Ali" was a shop set in a houseboat. There were exquisite pashmina shawls with typical Kashmiri chain-stitch embroidery. Shaku was asked to take off her wedding band and a 'shatoosh' shawl of gossamer threads, was pulled through to prove its authenticity. Shaku was fascinated but could not afford the price. These shawls were banned in India as too many deer had to be slaughtered to get the soft chest down for a single piece. In Srinagar, every shop-keeper worth his salt, could produce a couple. She draped one across her shoulders. It felt as soft as a new born baby's fuzz, was light as a feather and comfortably warm. She settled for a white coat, embroidered all over with different coloured chinar leaves.

It was with regret that they caught the bus out of town. The previous night there had been a fire fight between the troops and militants holed up in a two storey, wooden house by the lake. They heard the sound of gun shots but thought it to be a wedding celebration. The militants, all three of them, were killed after a fierce battle. The owner, his wife and two year old son were wounded and taken to the Sheikh Abdullah Hospital. The family had been held hostage and were lucky to be alive, for they could easily have been killed by the militants or the soldiers.

"Can you imagine if Luv or Khush were in a similar situation? These people go through it daily! Why isn't anyone trying to bring peace to the valley?"

Mustapha explained, "It is not that simple. You plant a chinar and it grows tall and straight with proper care. You stop nurturing it, and it becomes stunted, ugly, its branches like twisted, diseased limbs. The people of Kashmir withered at the hands of greedy politicians who refused to nurture the tree. Pakistan, who always envied India this jewel, stepped in and started manuring the stunted tree. The tree grew but the branches still looked stunted and ugly. It is too late. There will have to be desperate measures to bring back the chinar's glory. India will have to manure it well to restore the lost magnificence of the valley of flowers."

"They need education and jobs to get them out of this morass. Isn't that so Hakim?"

"And tolerance too. We need to forget religion, our varied cultural back grounds and ancient beliefs to bring back the trust everyone has lost. When a man or woman is frisked ten times a day, the chinar will wither." He quoted his father.

Shaku was thoughtful. "And yet if there is no tight security, many more lives will be lost. Perhaps Kashmir needs men like Commando to enforce some rules and fill their empty stomachs."

It was a thought worth chewing on. The little group was silent as it rode into the Himalayas on the rickety bus.

- -

Zakir was furious. He sat before his mother Zarina, as she cooked the evening meal. "Abba said I wanted to be a hero. I want to become a 'shaheed,' a martyr for the Cause, not some filmy hero!"

"There, there!" his mother soothed him. "You are but a child. We love you and this boat is yours. Why would you want to become a shaheed?"

"The Cause is far greater than all of us. We have been slighted, become second class citizens in a state which should have been independent and ours. And you talk of my inheriting a house boat! I want to inherit the land!" The boy's eyes were red with anger.

"I don't know who fills your head with such garbage! Don't you want to grow up and have a beautiful bride who will look after your parents too?"

"I shall have many 'houris' if I become a shaheed. My teacher has told me so."

Did he get the message from above or did the Pakistani government send it?" Zarina laughed.

"Don't make fun of the Cause, Ammi. They might issue a fatwa against you."

"Who are 'they?' Why do 'they' live in the shadows? Why do 'they' not fight face to face?"

"How can you forget Dadajaan? Who were the men who killed him?"

"The sniper did!"

"That's not what I heard. Dadajaan told me a lot of things. They were after him."

"Who?"

"The Indian soldiers. They made it look like an accident. My teacher says it was well planned."

That night Zarina spoke of her fears to Abdullah. "They may influence our son and take him away from us. Try and send him to college. He might forget the Cause."

But her husband was not so sure. The clandestine teachers fired children with promises of glory, cash and a paradise inhabited by houris. For any fifteen year old it was a dream worth having.

Little did Abdullah realize that Zakir had found a metal biscuit tin under the floor-boards in the dining room. They had the names and addressses of guests dating back four decades. Hakim and Shaku were on the list as was a man called Commando.

- -

Amina Bi and Mustapha were exhausted by the time they reached Kandahar. Shaku looked around her through the net strip of her burkha. Her mother-in-law was enveloped in a similar gown. She was shocked at the change that had come over Afghanistan. The bright blue burkhas of yester-year were not to be seen anywhere. Even in the various buses they had taken, there were no women travelers, just men in drab clothes, sporting long beards and black turbans. When Hakim tried to strike a conversation with one of them, the man turned his head away to look at the barren, bombed out landscape. No one smiled or chatted, or carried baskets of vegetables and eggs, or chickens strung across their shoulders. Suddenly, all of Kandahar had lost its energy, brilliant colours and the loud cries of hawkers selling their wares. Many of the men on the bus clasped guns between their knees. Hakim with his clean shaven face, felt naked and exposed.

He vowed he would not shave till they were back in Jullundur. "Are they the Taliban?" Shaku whispered into his ear. He shushed her, indicating that they were watched by men who did not approve of women talking openly to their men.

Mustapha shaded his eyes against the bright sun and fine dust and looked into the distance. He was agitated. "Where are they?" he asked no one in particular.

"Who?" asked Amina Bi.

"My cousins Jalal, Tariq and Ahmed and their wives. They were here to meet us last time. Why have they not come?"

The question remained unanswered as a cloud of dust heralded the bus that was to take them to the village of Khas. Hakim helped his parents on. The road was much worse than on their last visit. In the distance they could see the huddle of mud coloured huts, but instead of bright yellow mustard fields, there were acres of red, pink and white poppies swaying violently in the wind.

There was an eerie silence in the bus, unlike the joyful chatter they had heard during their last visit. Surrounded by sullen men, bumping along a non-existent road, Shaku felt very alone. She wondered if this area too came under Commando's influence? The remoteness of the place did not seem to support such an idea.

She was sure now that he was in the drug trade. His "pharmaceutical business" was a part of the poppy fields before her. But did he have the power or clout to control any of these armed rustics sitting around her?

There was a sudden jolt as the bus hit a boulder. Then silence. The engine was dead. The driver and cleaner got down and crawled under the vehicle. The odour of diesel filled the air. Black liquid stained the road. "We cannot go further," the driver declared.

"What should we do?" asked Hakim.

"Walk or wait for another bus."

"When is it due?"

"Who knows… today, tomorrow or the day-after."

"But I have my aged parents with me," said Hakim, obviously distressed.

One of the armed men laughed mirthlessly, "You should not be travelling with the aged and women. Leave them at home. That's where they belong."

A surge of anger arose in Hakim's throat. He whipped around towards the speaker but Shaku's restraining hand on his arm, warned him. Hakim looked down and then helped Mustapha and Amina Bi to come down the steps.

They sat for a long while, on boulders lying by the side of the road, their baggage strewn around them. The young men had walked on, quite used to the breakdown of vehicles. As the shadows lengthened, Shaku saw some donkeys ambling towards them. They were carrying bricks for a resident at Khas. Hakim offered fifty Indian rupees if the man would take the old couple. After a lot of haggling, four hundred was agreed upon. Mustapha and Amina Bi sat on rope panniers loaded with bricks. By nightfall they reached the first house at Khas.

The brick man took them straight to Ahmed's house. A mere chink was opened and Hakim saw his uncle's face, framed by the dim light of a hurricane lamp. Almost surreptitiously, the old man gestured them in. He put a finger to his lips, indicating that there should be no noisy greetings or loud talk.

"What has happened?" whispered Mustapha. "Why were you not at the bus stand?"

"The walls have ears," Tariq told him. "The whole of Khas knows you are coming. They were sent a message four days ago." Shaku realized that they had left Srinagar that many days earlier.

"So what?" whispered Amina Bi, her face puckered with fatigue and whitened by a powdery dust.

"Behan! Sister! This is not the Afghanistan you knew. Everything has changed. We have to be careful," said Jalal. Hakim and Shaku were aware that many eyes watched them but they had nothing to do with Commando.

Jehan and Aziza came in. They hugged their women guests, chatted excitedly but with lowered voices. Washed and in fresh clothes, the family sat down to eat.

"Jehan Bhabi, have you any news of my family?" asked Amina Bi.

"There is a family with that name, at a village to the south-east, near the Pakistan border. It is a full day's journey by pony or ox-cart. People usually walk the distance but I don't think you should attempt that."

"Do you know the name of the village?"

"Something like Dost or Dast. I'm not sure."

Amina Bi's face brightened. She turned to Mustapha, "I have to go there before we return to Jullundur. Supposing my brother and sister are still alive?"

Her husband and son doubted it but this trip was mainly for Amina Bi's sake. If they could trace her family, their promises would be fulfilled.

The morning was crisp and bright. Shaku helped Aziza fetch water from the well. Curious glances were thrown at them, but Shaku had been warned not to enter into any conversation. The morning meal over, they hung their blue robes and the two young women sat down to talk in Aziza's room.

"You are still not married? Why?"

"Marry!" Aziza was bitter and sarcastic. "Who do I marry? Those people who travelled with you? The Taliban tells us who to marry. They give us no choice. We have to produce children for the Cause."

Shaku put her arms around the girl's shoulders and hugged her tight.

"Have you been doing the English work I set you?"

Aziza climbed a stool and brought out the copy books hidden in the rafters. "I finished the work a long time ago, but you did not come, so I went on repeating it. I understand a little English now," she said with pride.

"What about speech? Do you listen to the BBC news?"

"We are not allowed to do so. Even possessing a radio can earn us a flogging."

Shaku looked down and held her head in her hands. Whatever she had heard or seen to date, was far removed from any visions of an educated society of women, surging forth on the road to independence and enlightenment. The women of her dreams were empowered to lead others towards a better world, which jostled new ideas and taught them to their children. The reality was a glimpse of Dante's Inferno. The Taliban was pushing its women to the brink of primeval subsistence. By not allowing girls' schools and colleges, the existing world would shrink and a few men could then train their children to think single mindedly about the Cause. Was this Huxley's 'Brave New World' or Hitler's poster of ethnic purity? To Shaku it seemed a fusion of both.

She looked into Aziza's eyes. "I shall teach you as much as I can and write out pages of words, sentences and stories. I may never be able to return to Afghanistan but you will have learnt something. Be brave and pass your knowledge on to others."

The younger woman nodded. Her eyes brimmed over with tears.

"Bring me a lot of paper and pencils. We shall start tonight."

"Didi, you must not speak of this to anyone... not even to Bhai, or our lives will be in great danger."

"How will you get the paper? I shall need at least two reams." said Shaku.

"I have my sources. A little boy, who thinks he loves me, will do anything at all for me. I shall meet him when it is dark."

Two days later, with a pile of paper and several pencils, Shaku restarted Aziza's left off education. They worked in the wee hours of the morning and well into the night. Jehan grumbled that oil for the lamps was getting over too fast but she attributed it to the ragged wick and asked Tariq to trim it.

- -

CHAPTER XV

"To die for the truth is not to die merely for one's faith, or one's country; it is to die for the world. Their blood is shed in confirmation of the noblest claim... the claim to feed upon immortal truth, to walk with God, and be divinely free."... Cowper.

A FIELD OF POPPIES.

A mountain range and many borders away, Commando sat flipping through the news channels. Another attempt had been made to assassinate the President of Afghanistan, Hamid Karzai. He escaped but many of his security guards were killed or wounded.

Karzai worked from a fortress, virtually under siege by the ever expanding Taliban. American troops guarded him and seldom let him out of sight. He was the symbol of democracy, a brave man, to be used as long as he served a purpose. If he travelled out of the country, they escorted him to the helicopter and buzzed around his craft till he crossed the borders of Afghanistan and Pakistan. He made his speeches and pleas on world platforms and hoped that his voice was heeded. He knew the world could not understand his people or the age old rules they lived by. Nations who decried the use of burkhas could not possibly comprehend the safety it afforded. Afghanistan kept its women safe from rape and its milder forms, eve-teasing and molestation. Like the Soviets, the USA did not know how to deal with the proudest, most fierce ethnic group in the world.

After Massoud's murder followed by 9/11, America turned towards Iraq, a symbol of oppression and selfishness; a scapegoat that could be sacrificed without too much of an outcry. There was not a scrap of evidence to show that Saddam had anything to do with the destruction of the Twin Towers. Nations willingly turned a blind eye to the web of deceit they were proffered, as long as their supplies of oil were secure. Iraq guaranteed those supplies. Afghanistan promised only blood, tears and sacrifice. That one single war turned the tide of modern history. No longer did Muslims belong to this or that country. No longer did they speak different languages. They were one under the banner of Islam.

"The moderates are being snuffed out." Commando made this observation to Renuka who sat knitting a sweater for a winter baby that swelled her belly. "That one war pushed Muslims to one side, the rest of the world to the other. Today we lump them together adding to the alienation of the moderates. No one will listen and the atrocities keep mounting."

"Don't let it worry you. You always behaved equally and fairly with everyone. No one shall harm us."

"Have you wondered what gives them the courage to blow themselves up? A lad of twelve, straps dynamite to his torso and blows himself up in a crowded market. A mere boy can kill hundreds with a smile on his lips. Look at me! I am afraid of falling on the road! What gives them so much courage and for what? A soldier who goes to war and faces the enemy displays the same guts. Who is the enemy... the soldier or the so called terrorist? It just depends on who you define as your enemy. The same fence divides them both. It is like cash. Place it in a bank and it is white. Keep it in a 'matki,' a mud pot, buried underground and it becomes black. Whatever its colour, it buys the same soaps and dals."

Renuka realized something was on her husband's mind. She went to the kitchen and ordered a nimboo paani for him. The sugar always helped calm him down.

The next day, Commando lost contact with the two men who were keeping an eye on the little group that was travelling in Afghanistan. There were no messages, no phone calls, no couriers, nobody, just silence from a dark, dusty corner of the globe.

"I have to go on business," he told Renuka.

"Where... and how long will you be?"

"The usual... give or take a week or two. You know me, I never stray from home," he teased, winking at her.

"Will you be back before the baby arrives? There are just four weeks to go." Renuka knew she would get no definite answer but she had to ask.

Commando left in the middle of the night, racing away in the jeep that carried him towards the Pakistan border. As always, he travelled alone. All along the way he spoke to his contacts. After Kandahar, there was no news at all. He left the jeep with a drug runner and crossed the border into Pakistan on foot, a palm sized, state of the art pistol strapped to his left ankle. They knew him well for he was generous with his money and had rehabilitated many villagers affected by firing from both sides, across no man's land. For Commando a human being had no nationality. His own wealth was for all to share. The largesse he distributed made it easier for him to travel to forbidden areas.

"I have brought you a burkha. Put it on... it will be easier for you to get to Khas. The Taliban rule the country side. They will not touch a woman in a burkha. Rashid will travel with you." Khan Bahadur had his shepherd's hut near the border, on the edge of a meadow, where his huge flock of sheep were allowed to graze. He was also the biggest drug dealer in the area. Commando and he had known each other since the honeymoon on the Taj Mahal. They had implicit trust in each other.

Rashid was one of Khan Bahadur's most trusted Afghani lieutenants. He accompanied Commando in the guise of a jealous, gun-toting husband. It was not difficult to piece together the route the family had taken. They asked questions from trusted men. Yes, the little group from Jullundur had passed that way. They followed, using the same modes of transportation. Their clues lay amongst bus drivers, tonga men, donkey owners. As expected, at Kandahar the trail went cold. Commando felt a slab of ice land on his heart. It was at a brick kiln, on the out-skirts of town, that they gathered credible information. The owner led them to a labourer who ferried bricks to the surrounding villages. The man described a group of two men and two women. The old woman and her husband were too tired to walk. He had taken them to a house at Khas, seated on the panniers of his brick laden donkeys. The younger couple had walked the distance.

Rashid asked, "Are they still there?"

"I don't think so. I heard they left for a village called Dost two days ago."

Commando and his companion took the next bus to Dost.

- -

When Amina Bi heard about the family at "Dost" or "Dast," she was most excited. "They could be my family! Imagine meeting Habiba and Daud after so many years... and their children and grand children! I won't even be able to recognize them."

"Suppose it is a different family? Is there no way of finding out?" Hakim asked Tariq.

"We could but it would take some time. You are welcome to stay and move once we know for sure," answered the old man.

Shaku knew that they were already straining the household economy by their visit. As per the rules of hospitality, Mustapha's cousins were producing the best fare they could afford. More days would cause immense scarcity of commodities which were not easily available.

"Hakim, you take Ammi and Abba to meet the family. I would like to stay here for a few more days to spend time with Aziza."

Hakim did not want to leave her behind nor could he allow his parents to travel alone through such rough and dangerous terrain.

In the end it was Tariq's wife Jehan who made the decision for them. "Shaku is a person who my daughter relates to. She may be able to persuade Aziza into making a happy marriage. The three of you can go it alone and pick Shaku up on your way back. She is safe here with us."

Dawn saw the trio take off in a covered ox-cart, towards an unknown village. Little did Jehan realize that her daughter wanted Shaku around for more than just chatting and discussing her future marriage.

The two girls wasted no time in getting on with writing and preparing lessons.

"Education is the key to your freedom Aziza," Shaku assured her pupil. "Someday if you can go to college, you can earn a degree. That degree will allow you to work. You will earn a salary and marry only if you want to. It is not a compulsion. A woman who has no money has no freedom or respect."

"Didi, the Taliban is closing all schools and colleges for girls. There were many schools for girls, constructed by an American in the border towns. I hear the Taliban has burnt them all and told the girls to stay at home."

"Such a repressive regime cannot stay forever," countered Shaku. "Their ideas would be a threat to world peace. Countries are very advanced in science, health, agriculture and education. You have to see the other side Aziza, to believe it. Even my country, in-spite of its shortcomings and lack of good governance, is forging ahead in a million fields. If things ease up, you can come and stay with Hakim and me. We shall introduce you to the new world. The free world will not allow the Taliban to exist, of that I am sure."

Shaku described the Basti School to her young friend. She told her of the slum children who were taught every subject so that they could shift to the best schools in town. From there they could compete with their peers and move on into a world of equal opportunity. If families did not earn enough but could get scholarships for their children, there would be a window opening into a better, more financially secure world.

"And Aziza, countries are vying with each other in offering scholarships to the best young minds. In this fashion their pool of the best brains is replenished. In India, poor children through better education, are forging ahead as compared to those who do not have to strive at all because they rely on their parents wealth."

Aziza's eyes shone as she looked into a future that could possibly be hers. Shaku and she read late into the night.

- -

The burkha clad woman and her burly husband reached Dost late in the evening. They talked to several people and knocked on many doors before they found the three travelers, sitting in the midst of a new found family.

Burkha off, a worried look on his face, Commando's first question was, "Where is Madamji?"

Hakim told him about Shaku's insistence on staying back at Khas, for Aziza's sake.

Commando pulled Hakim to one side of the room and whispered, "We must go back before dawn breaks." It was an order not a suggestion.

"What is the matter?" Hakim was afraid for Shaku.

"Come outside. I do not want to alarm the old people or ruin their evening."

The two young men, wrapped in thick woolen shawls, knees drawn up to their chins, sat on the mud floor, against the wall of the house. They had chosen the darkest corner of the compound. Rashid, also wrapped against the chill wind, stood surveying the landscape around them.

Commando told Hakim of the journey that began three days earlier. He described the Cause and its soldiers. He talked about young men and women who laid down their lives with a smile on their lips. He talked about a house boat named Taj Mahal and Bashir who was shot in an "encounter." He talked about Bashir's grandson Zakir, who was a part of the Cause and privy to a biscuit tin with the names and addresses of all those who had stayed on the house boat. "But what has all this to do with us?" Hakim asked with visible impatience.

"Wait Bhai, wait! Try to understand what I am saying."

There were jobless, disgruntled youth who wanted some respect and would do anything to get it. There were nations let down by other nations, in spite of promises of aid and military backing. There were starving families, who, to feed their children, would accept the crumbs they were offered, never mind the source of those crumbs. There were politicians who were bent on leaving the poor where they were, because their empty bellies prevented them from revolting. There were others who played the religious card to make people insecure. There were bureaucrats who would not sign a paper till their palms were greased.

"This is the world we live in. This is the world where we choose the side we are going to be on. You have chosen one side, I, the other. Which is better, neither of us can say. But both lead to the same end. I want a comfortable life with food in my thaali. You too want the same thing but on your Royal Doulton dinner set."

So he had noticed! Hakim was all admiration for Commando. This evening had made it clear what Commando did. It was dangerous knowledge but it showed him the grey areas which dominate our lives and about which we can be so judgmental. "What about Shaku?" he asked and fear made his voice shake. She was the most precious being in his life.

"She is in great danger," said Commando softly. "We might be able to do something yet."

He told Hakim of the stationer at the village market. A little boy bought two reams of paper and a dozen pencils. Besides the good sale, the man found the incident strange. No one at Khas used so much paper. The boy's school provided its own stationery and girls were not supposed to get any 'taalim,' or education. Commando, who knew Madamji well, put two and two together. The inference was disturbing to both men.

"I have journeyed this far for her sake. We shall keep your parents here and leave well before dawn. My people have brought ponies. The journey should be short."

"Why can we not leave immediately?"

"We may lose our way. This is Taliban infested country."

- -

The house was quiet and completely dark, the silence broken by Tariq's gentle snores. A handful of pebbles hit the bolted wooden window in Aziza's room. Shaku heard it but turned over, pulling the quilt over her head. She thought it must be a cat chasing the bandicoots that lived in the rafters. There it was again, the same sound, pebbles against the wooden flaps of the window. She sat up and woke Aziza.

"Can you hear the sound of pebbles?"

Aziza shook her head and rubbed her eyes.

"There it is again!" Shaku lit the hanging lamp and put on her burkha. Aziza did the same.

The same whoosh and pebbles fell on the ground outside.

"Let's wake your parents," Shaku suggested.

"No let's not. It might be the cat. Let me see."

She opened the tower bolt and looked out. Strong, muscular hands grabbed her shoulders and dragged her out. Two men, their faces covered with the ends of their black turbans, leaped into the room and dragged Shaku out too. She tried to scream but a hand clamped down on her mouth, hard. She bit the hand and was slapped with brutal strength. Four men carried the two women into the poppy field. They set them down roughly and a fifth man asked, "Which of you has come from Hindustan?"

The girls were silent. Aziza started crying softly. One of the men hit her across the face. She fell flat on the ground and curled up in a fetal position, shielding her head against any further blows. The man raised his hand to hit her again. Shaku said, "I am from Hindustan."

The fifth man, who was obviously their leader, spoke in even, gentle tones. "We do not want your ideas here. We do not want you to corrupt our women. We are pure and want our women to be pure too."

Shaku looked at him defiantly through the net across her eyes. "You want to take away a woman's freedom. You want to make a slave out of her. You want to control the world by not letting people progress or get an education. You and your kind will not survive!"

One of the men pushed Shaku into a kneeling position. The leader, without the slightest hesitation, took out his pistol and shot her through the back of her head. Slowly, without a sound, she keeled over, onto the poppies, the blue burkha spread around her like a piece of the sky.

Aziza would not stop screaming but no one heard her. Two men held her down as the leader gave her fifty lashes with a cane. They left her unconscious in the field. The last words she heard before she passed out were, "Do not try to seek 'taalim.' You are as valuable and useful as the shoes on our feet. Consider yourself more than that and you too shall meet her fate."

They melted away in the darkness. Before they departed from the village they removed from the rafters, all the lessons Shaku had written for Aziza. Jehan and Tariq slept through the night till a neighbour's frantic knocking on their door, woke them in the morning. They had heard nothing. They carried Aziza home and laid her beside Shaku's body, on the floor. Then they removed their daughter's bloodied clothes, cleaned her and laid her to rest on the string bed. They sat by Shaku and keened.

The residents of Khas crammed Tariq's small courtyard. There was a stony silence made quieter by the muteness of children and babies, who too sensed that something terrible had occurred. Hardly anyone had spoken to the Indian woman who had landed in their midst for the second time. But the fact that one of their girls was brutally flogged and a woman guest murdered, threatened the foundations of Afghan hospitality. They had never had much more than that to offer. Many of them began questioning the value of Taliban rules, which till then had been accepted with resentment not out and out hostility. Shaku's death became a turning point in the thinking of ordinary individuals. The very thoughts the Taliban tried to suppress surged forward to make a village rise against them.

When Hakim and Commando saw the crowds, they were afraid. The people parted to let them through. Hakim looked at his beloved. She seemed asleep, none of the horror of the night before reflected on her face. A tiny hole in the forehead indicated that she was gone. She had often described a dream in which she had a hole in the forehead. Hakim cradled her head on his lap and ran his fingers along her lips. The crowds looked away, embarrassed by the very private, anguished and bewildered display of grief. Pathans never wore their hearts on their sleeve. It was considered a sign of weakness.

For the first time in adult memory, Commando cried. He wiped his eyes and nose with the back of his hand and strode out of the room, to do what he knew best... gathering information.

Shaku was cremated before sundown, as per the Hindu custom. As before, the residents of Khas turned up in full force. They helped collect the very scarce wood and brush for the pyre. By the following morning, her ashes were collected in an earthen 'matka,' for the long journey home. The headman requested some of the 'phool' or flowers of her remains for the village. They were handed over in a small container and buried in the poppy field at the same spot that was still stained by her blood. Khas built a stone memorial over it. The Taliban were aware of the new martyr they had unwittingly created. They watched the village and did not approve of its defiant thinking. They could not wipe out a community that was willing to die for its freedom. The initiative of self-destruction towards implementing the Cause was wrenched away from them by a young woman from Jullundur.

Aziza was conscious and quiet as Commando sat by her bedside. He wanted to know of the five men. Any detail, however insignificant, was important. She told him about Shaku's defiant words, her calmness and complete lack of fear, moments before she was killed. She told him how Shaku revealed her own identity so that they would not beat Aziza. "She even bit one of them on the hand."

Commando promised that he would send for Aziza and she would run the Basti School in Madamji's place. He could think of no better tribute to the Principal of the slum School.

As they rode towards Dost, Commando recounted Shaku's last moments to Hakim, who let the tears flow into a month old beard.

Mustapha and Amina Bi accepted Shaku's death with sorrow and characteristically resigned calmness. They were used to heart breaking losses. "It is Allah's will," said Mustapha.

"Her death will not be in vain," his wife said looking into the future.

- -

Kandahar was as drab and dusty as usual. At a chai shop, five men drank hot liquid out of earthen 'kujjas' or cups. They sat around a tin canister, used as a make shift stove to keep warm. They had removed the ends of the black turbans that normally covered their noses and mouths. All had dark, kohled eyes set in fair, handsome faces. One held his cup in the left hand for the right was bandaged. To one side of the room, a group of three men and two women in burkhas sipped hot tea. Commando watched the turbaned group through the net window over his eyes. He noticed the bandaged hand. He stood up and started moving towards them. Hakim too got up but was pushed back onto his stool by Rashid, who followed Commando. The men around the fire did not look at the burkhaed woman behind them. The leader threw a sheaf of papers into the burning embers, putting out his hands to warm them. At a sign from Commando, Rashid retrieved the papers. A familiar scrawl covered them. The five men had no time to pick up their guns, left carelessly and confidently with the shop owner who watched in stupefied silence at the unfolding scene. Not a sound was made, no one moved. Rashid pointed his gun and walked the men into the middle of the road where they were forced to kneel. Commando shot each one through the back of the head, his hands and weapon concealed under the voluminous burkha. The bullets burnt five neat holes in the silky, blue fabric.

The bus from Khas, on its return journey to Kabul, skirted the bodies and took on half a dozen passengers. Bodies were a common sight in rural Afghanistan where the Taliban dealt out swift justice. Questions were seldom asked, reasons seldom given. On the outskirts of a remote village, four men and an old woman got down to ride away on waiting horses, into the surrounding forest. The old woman sat behind one of the young men. They were never seen again.

CHAPTER XVI

"It is by education I learn to do by choice, what other men do by the constraint of fear."... Aristotle.

CLOSURE.

"Shaku's had a terrible accident." Hakim told Deepak and Pushpa over the phone. "We are bringing her home." They were all eating at a small 'dhaba' on the Indian side of the border. Commando had allowed no phone calls en-route as it could give their positions away. Rashid had gone back to Pakistan. Commando was amongst trusted friends. Deepak asked for more details. Hakim pretended the line was bad and said they would talk later.

- -

"I could not protect her!" Commando touched Deepak's feet and asked for forgiveness.

As he wept over Pushpa's sandals, she put her hand on his head and whispered, "We have lost a daughter but gained a son. Beta, you have a similar spirit within you. You shall

245

be the son we never had." Commando knew then that they did not blame him. He was to become a part of a family that had made Shaku the woman of substance that she was.

- -

Bari Kothi wore a pall of gloom as it conducted the last rites of a woman whose ashes were held within an earthen 'matka.' She was the child of the house, her spirit in every leaf and drop of water. The utter expressions of grief were over and done with. Inside, beating shocked hearts would be scarred forever.

"We must not show our grief to the children. We must make their lives normal. That's what Shaku would have wanted. We must never let them forget her ideals and courage." Deepak held Pushpa within the circle of his arms. She nodded through a veil of tears. Hakim sat with his children and told them how brave their mother was. Luv used a tissue to wipe the dampness from around his eyes. "I shall look after you Baba."

- -

In the years that followed, Commando's visits to the Bari Kothi multiplied. The school was renamed "Shakuntala Memorial Academy." Aziza became its Principal. Commando

The author and her husband